36 GEOMETRICAL PATTERNS FOR COLORNING

We live in fast times and taking a brake and few moments for ourselves can help reduce the stress and help the concentration.

This is not just coloring book it is way for you to do Visual Meditation.

Enjoy!

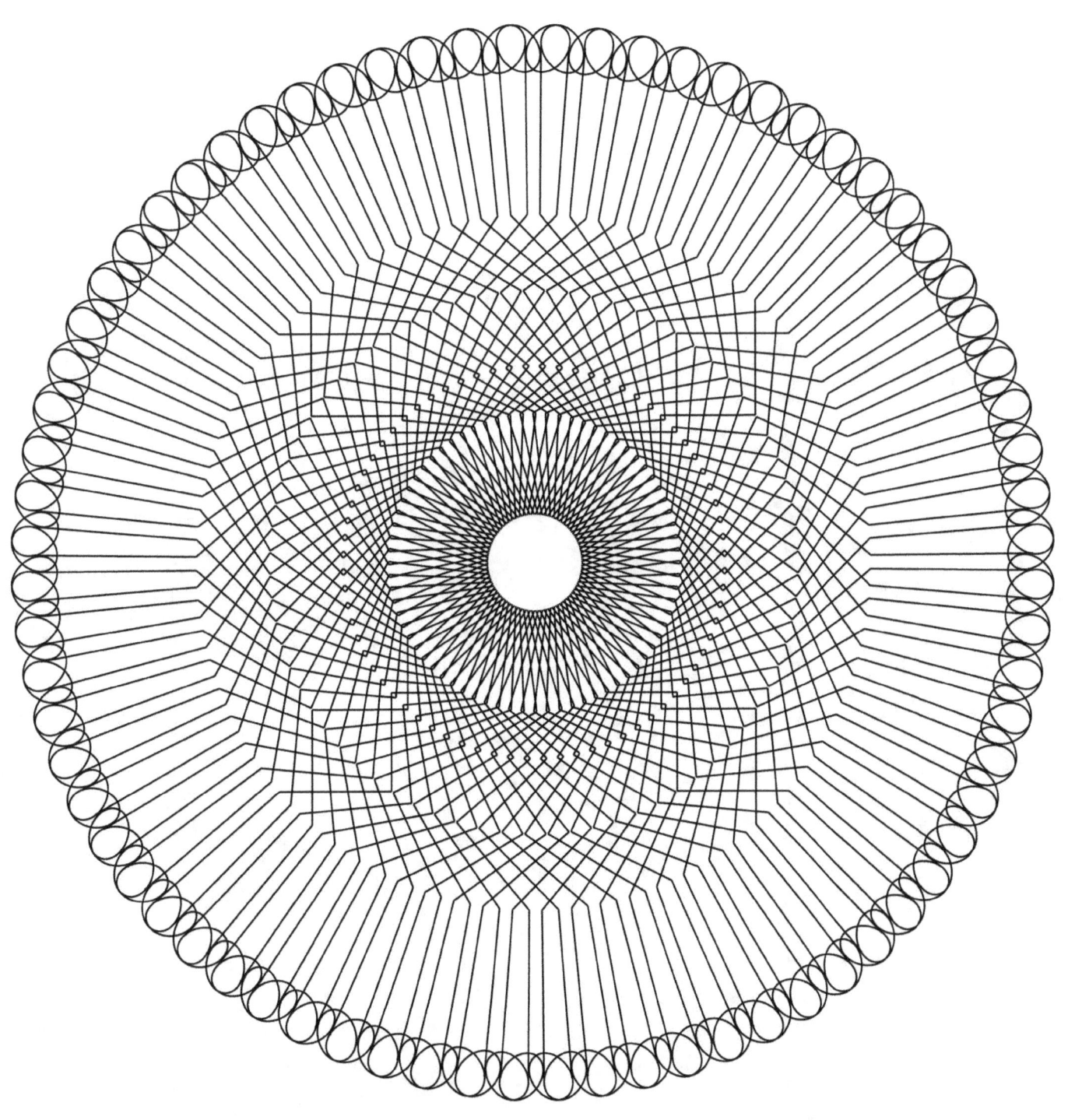

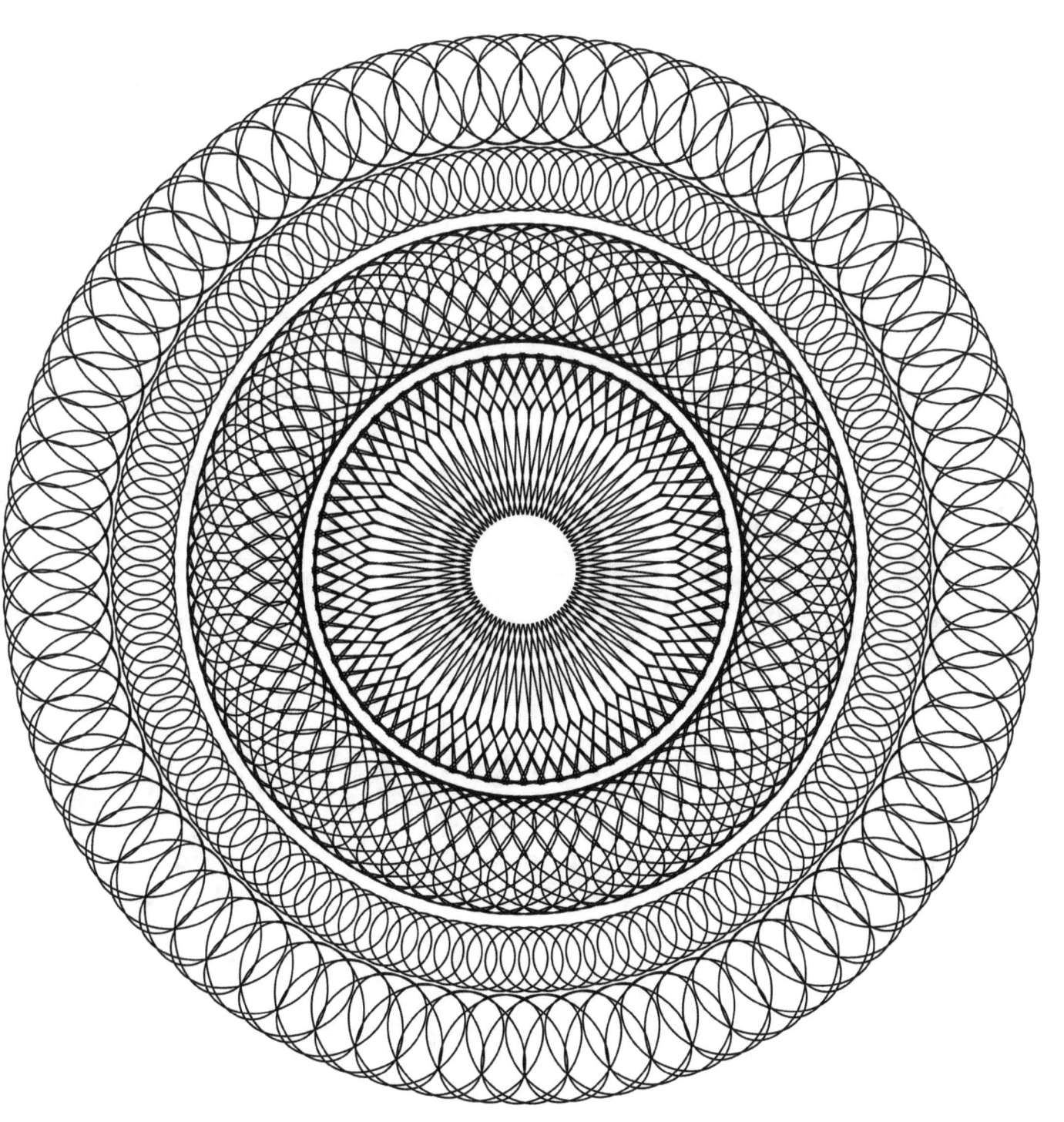

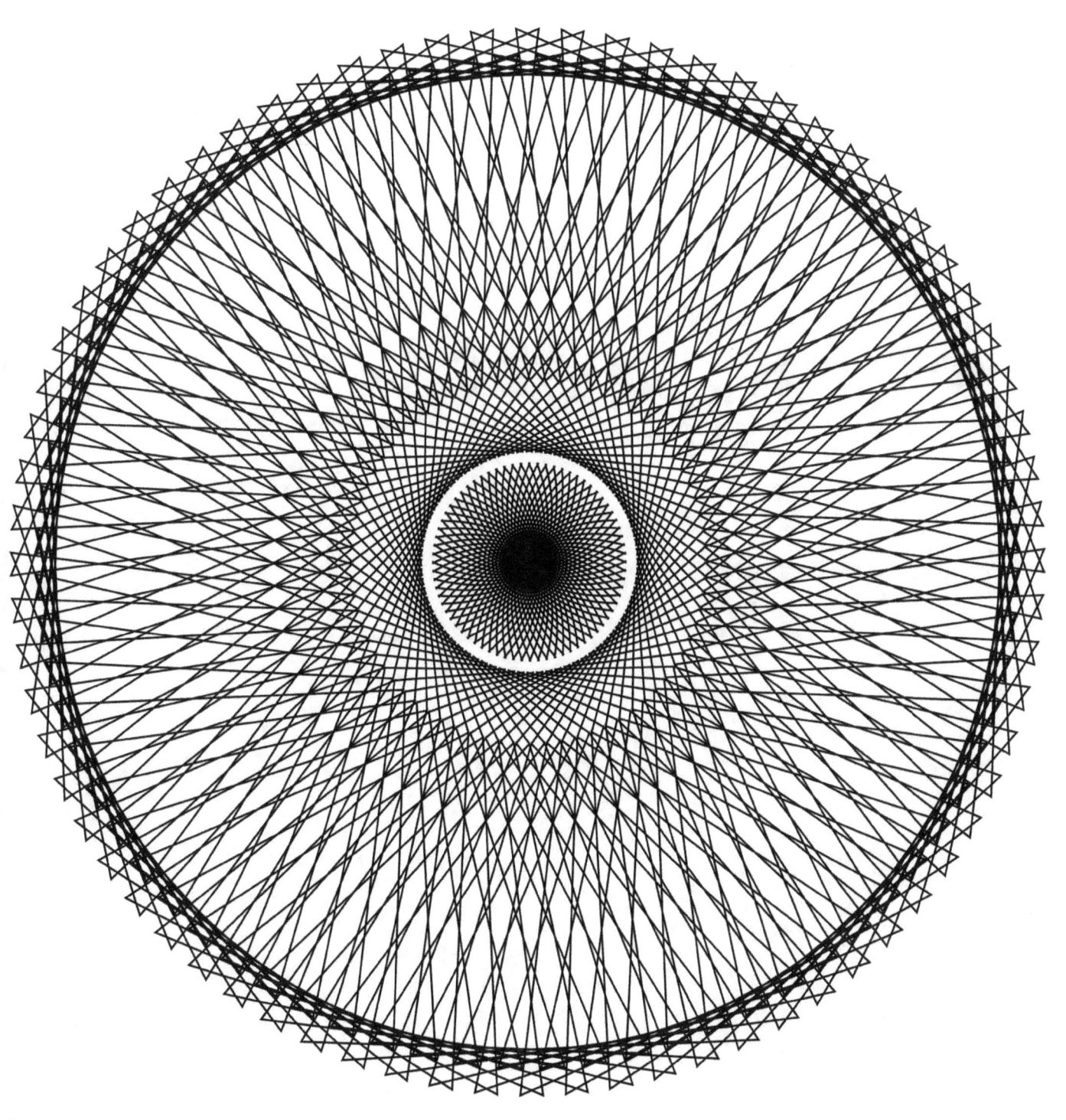

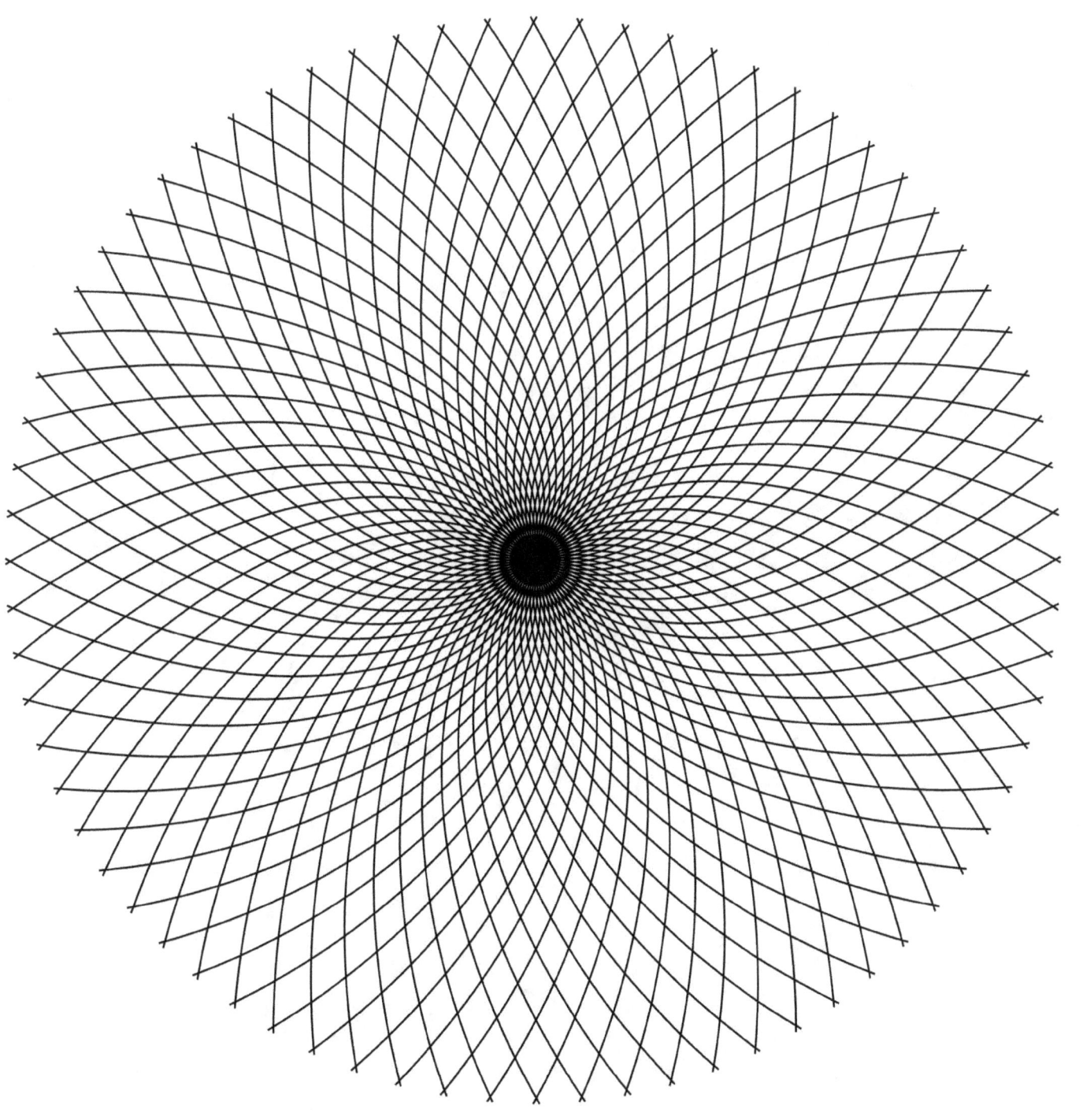

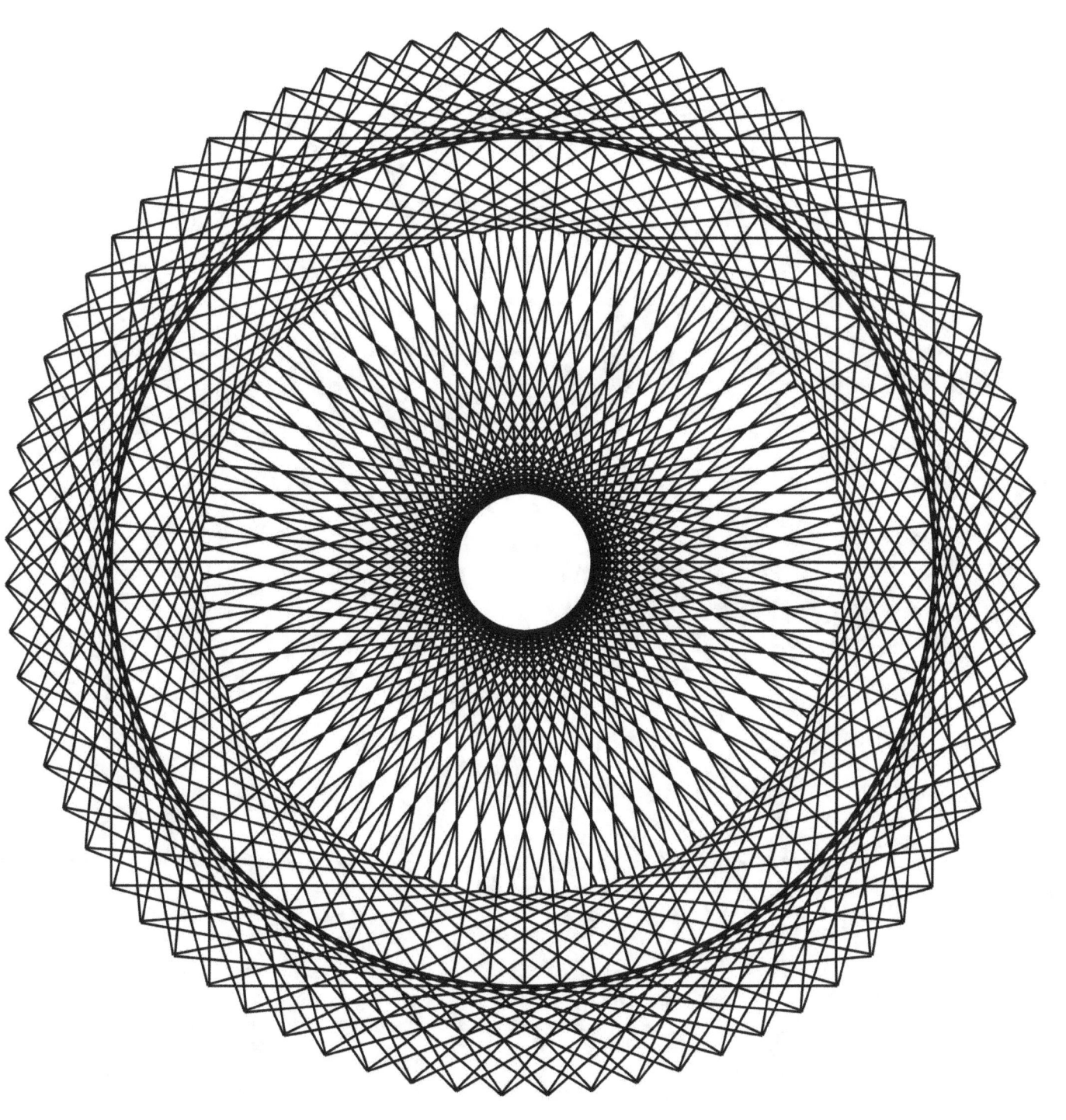

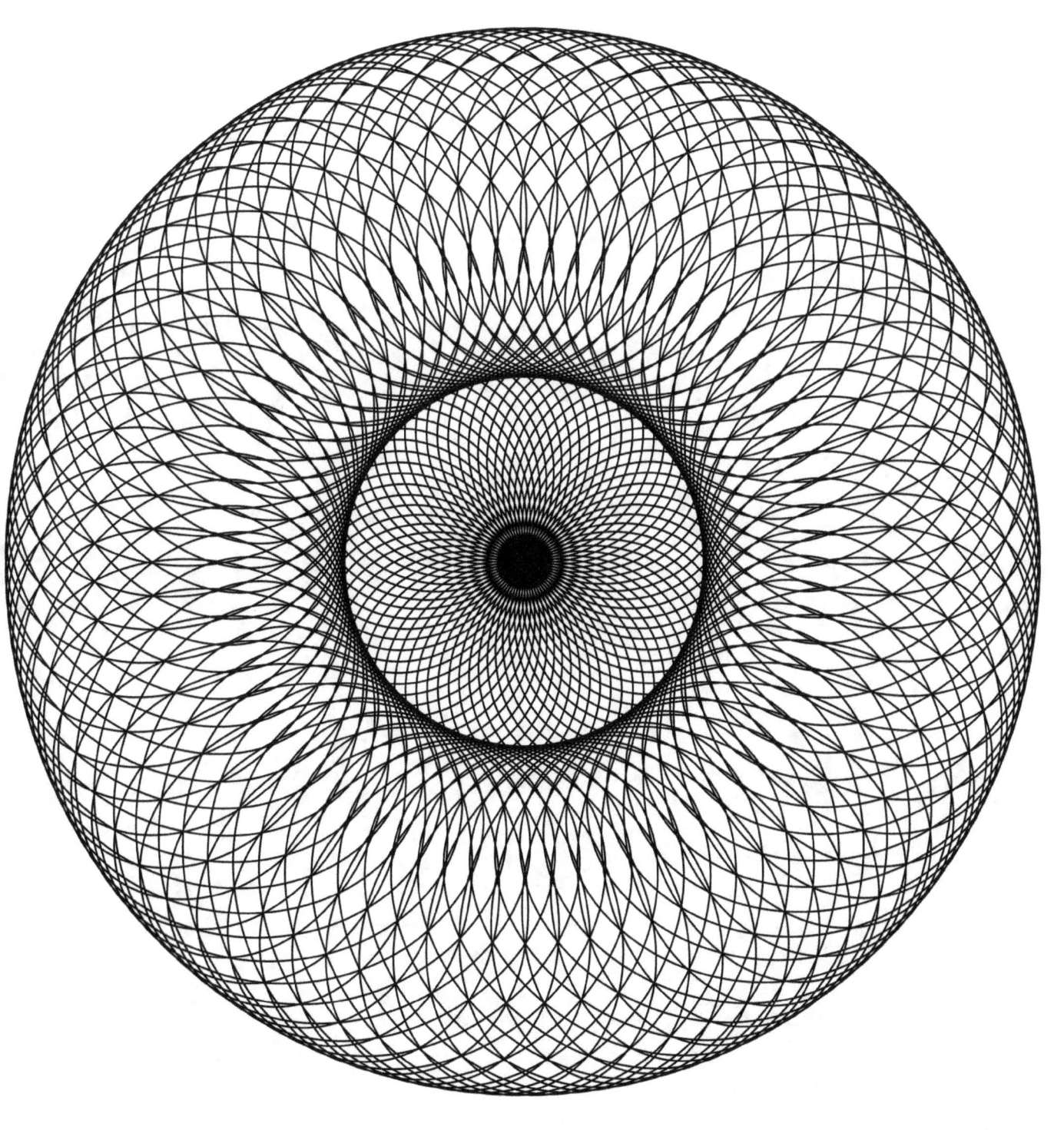

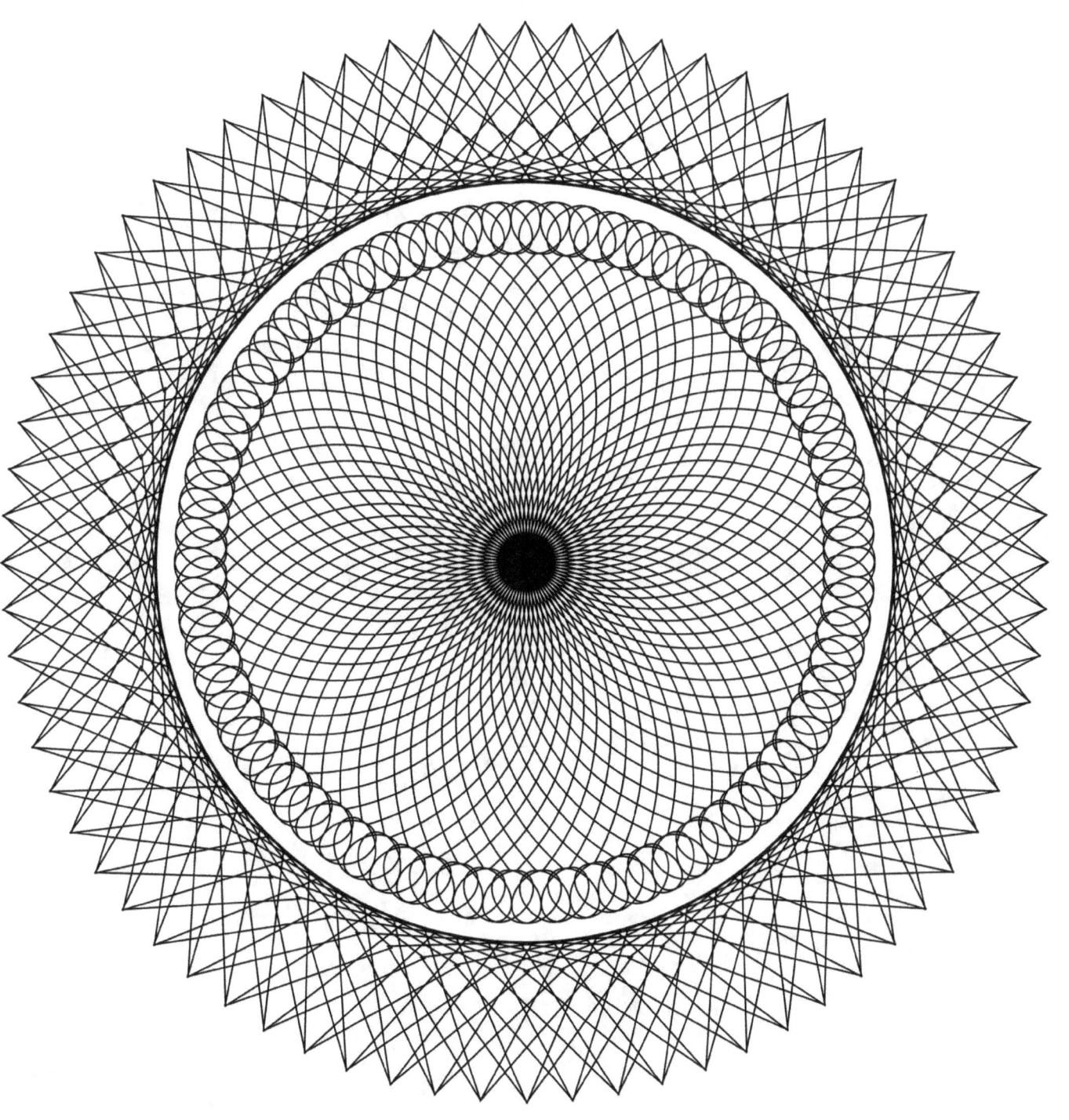

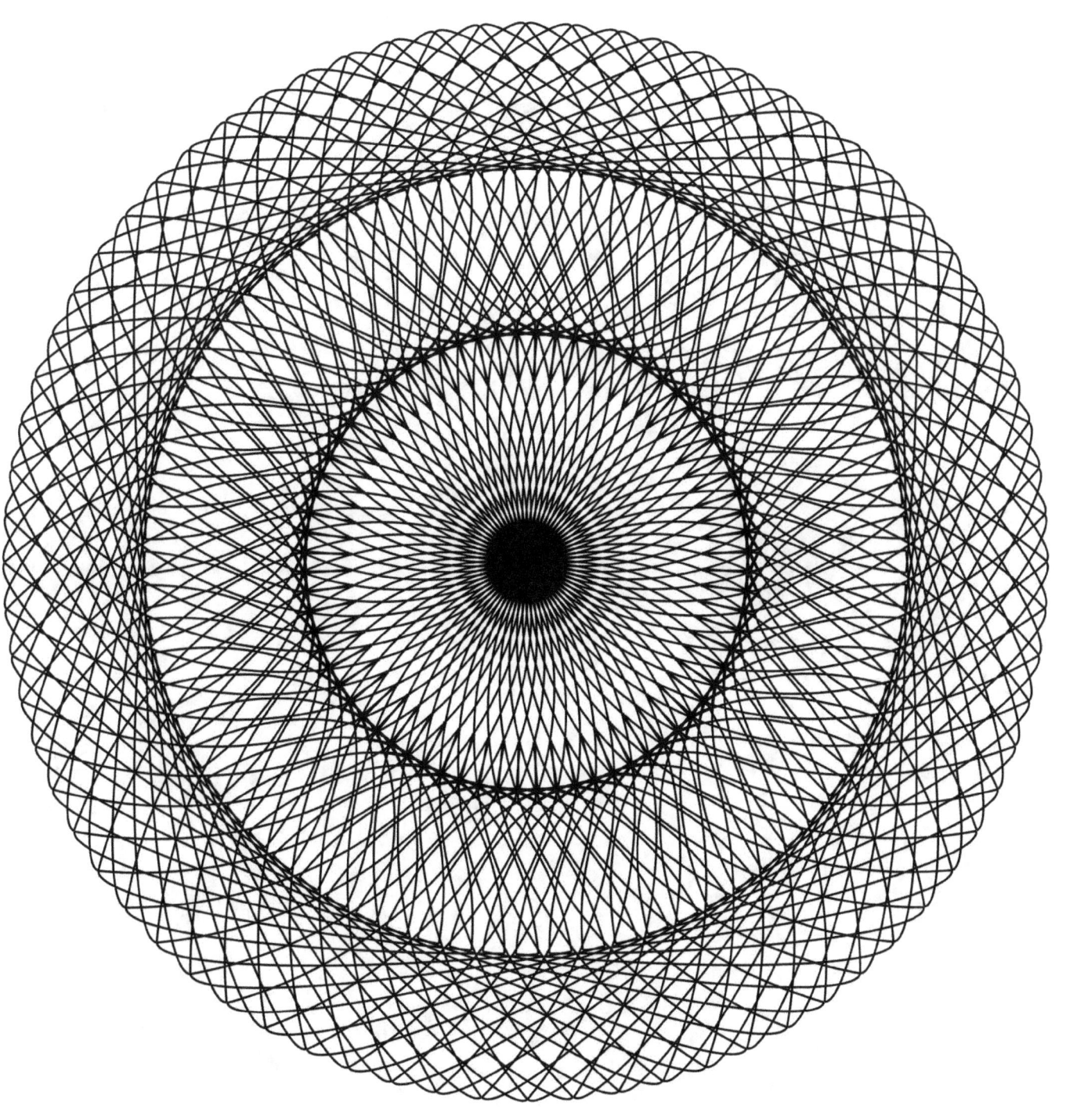

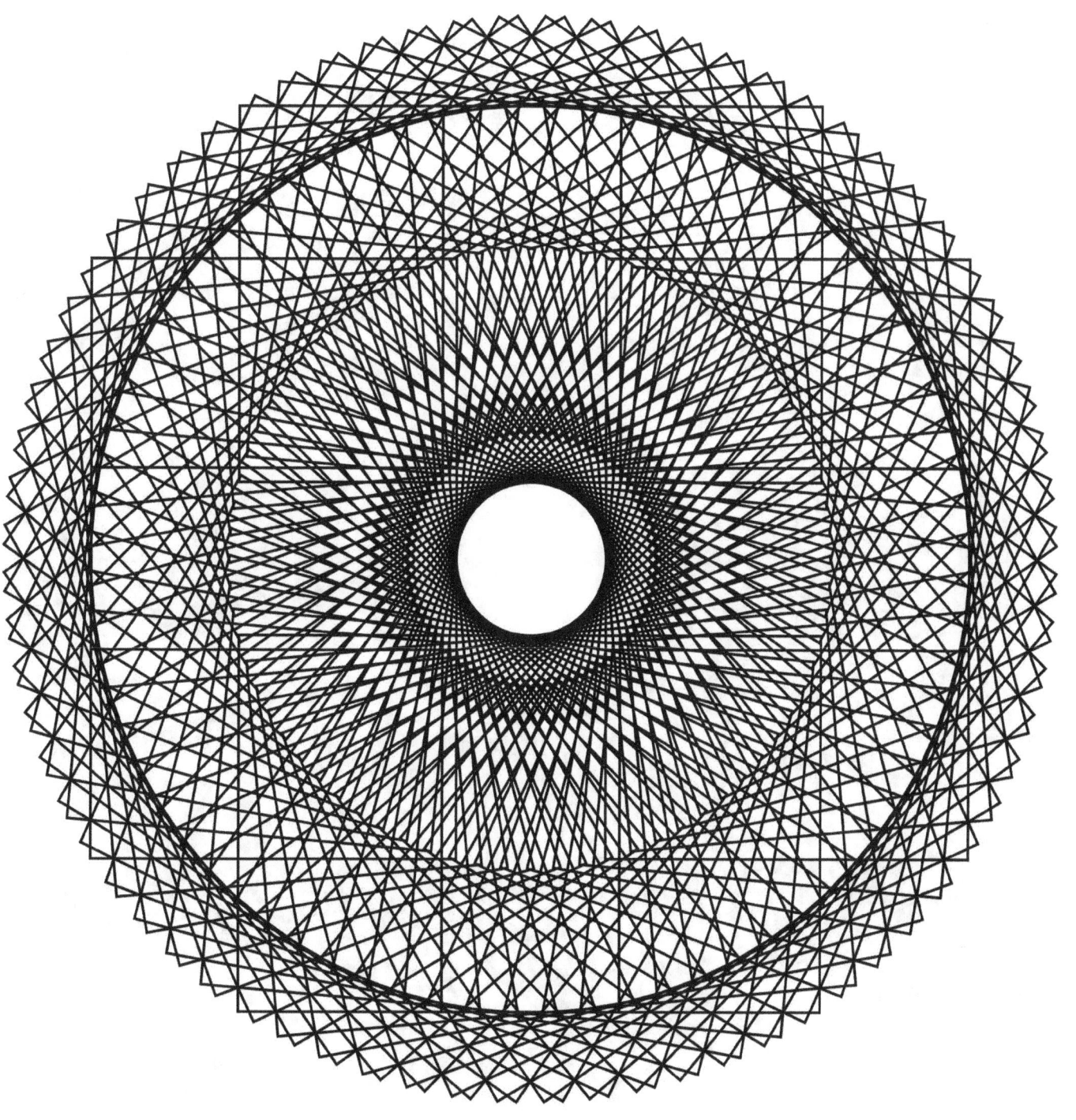

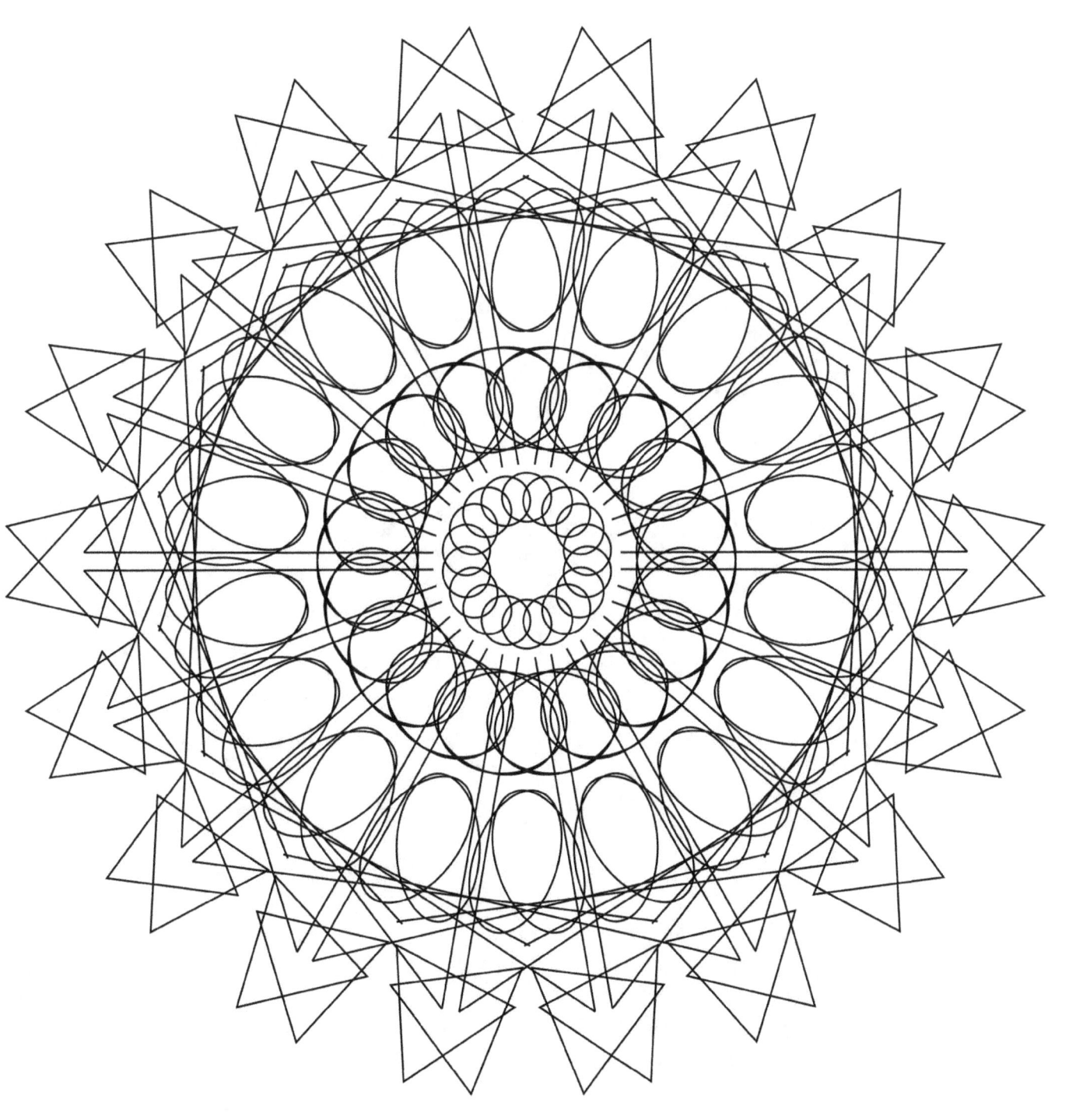

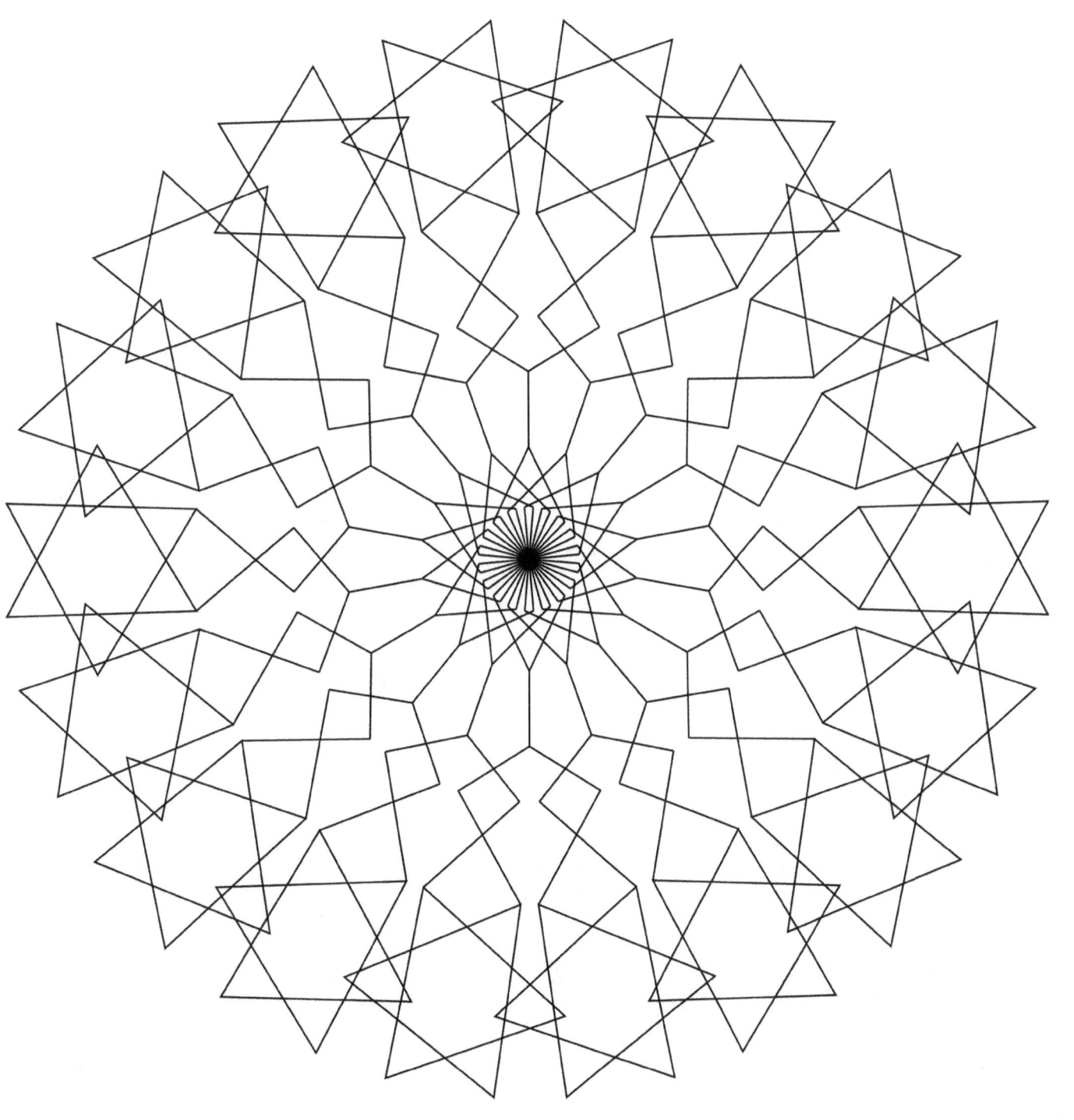

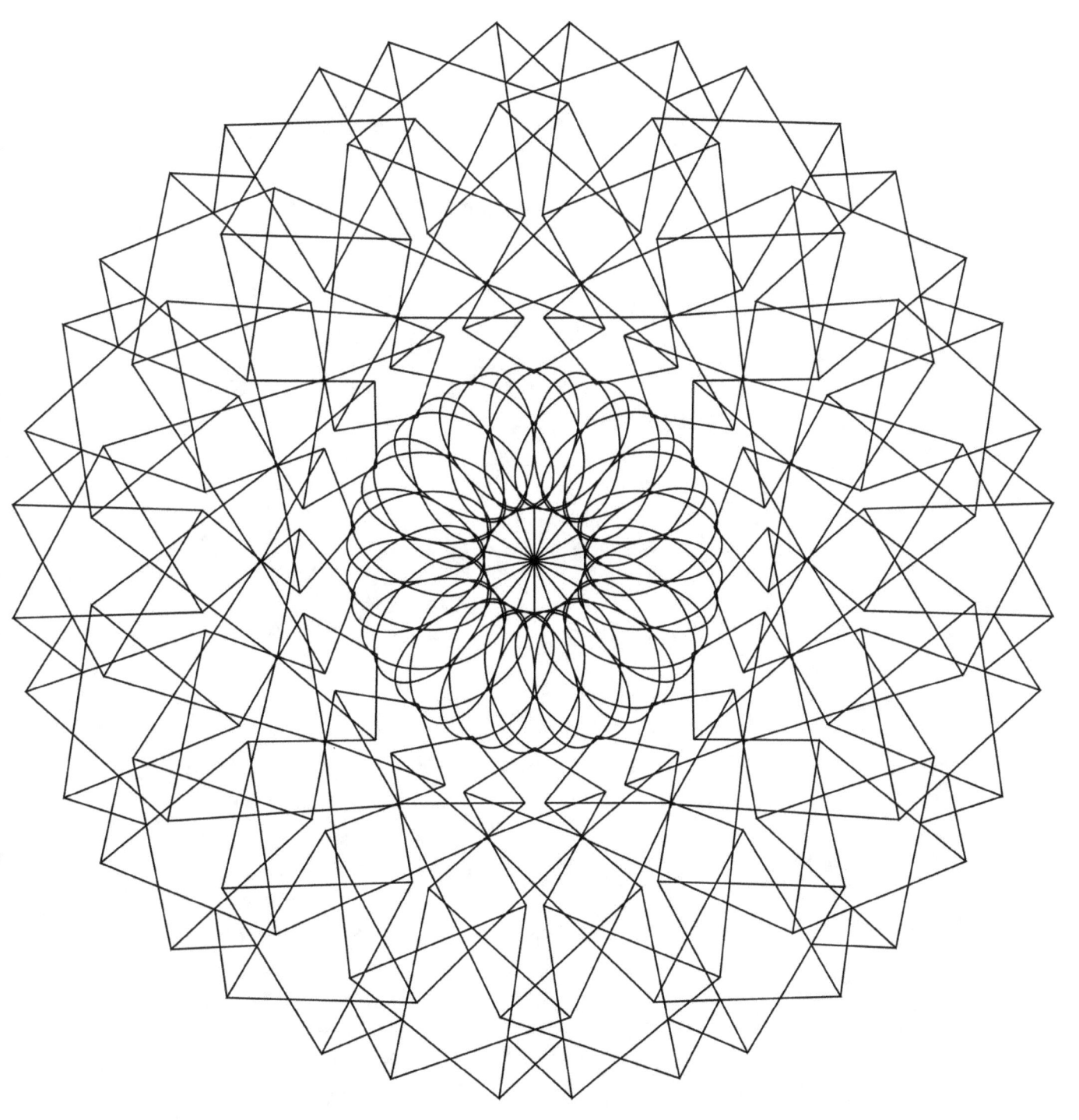

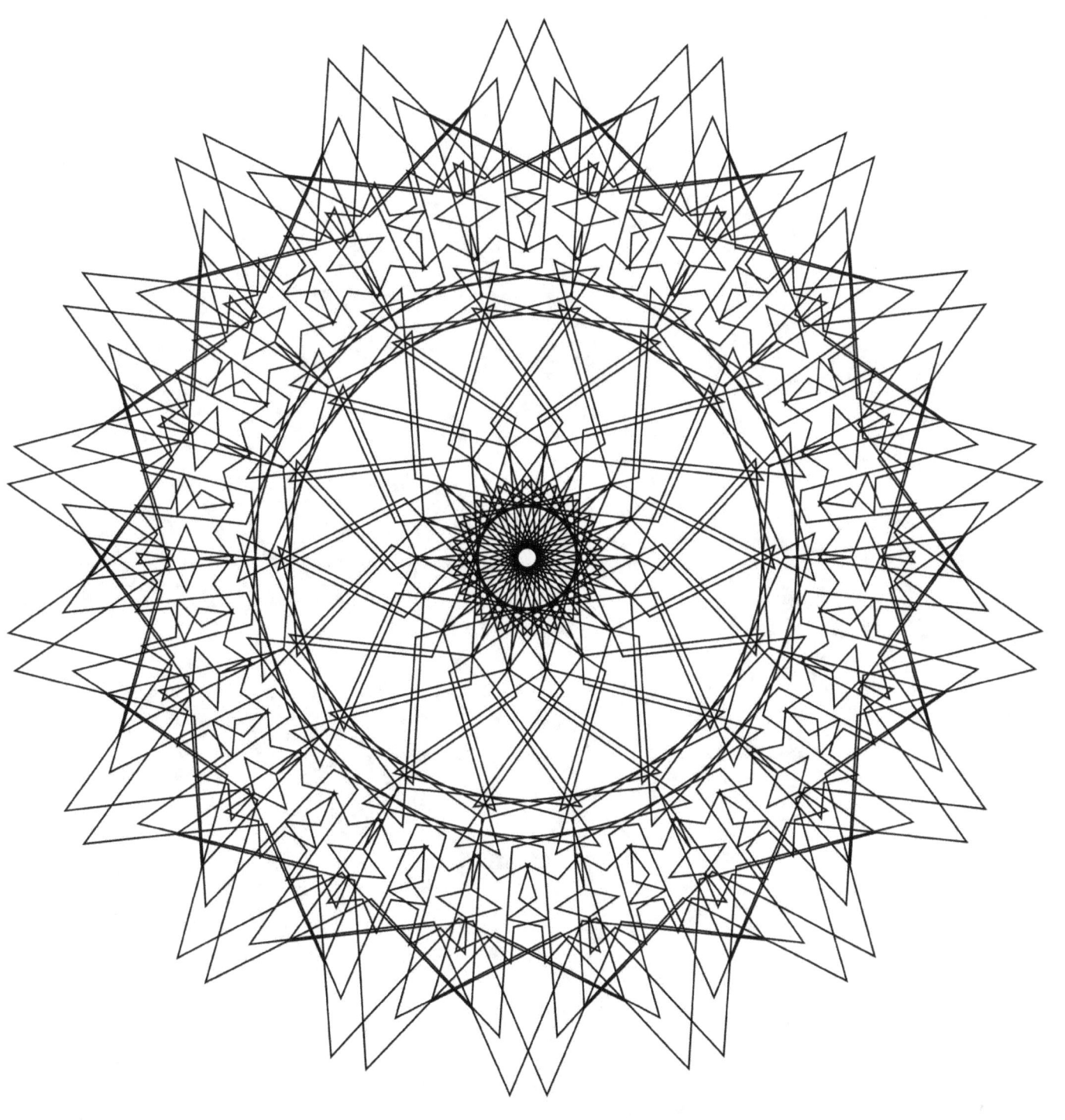

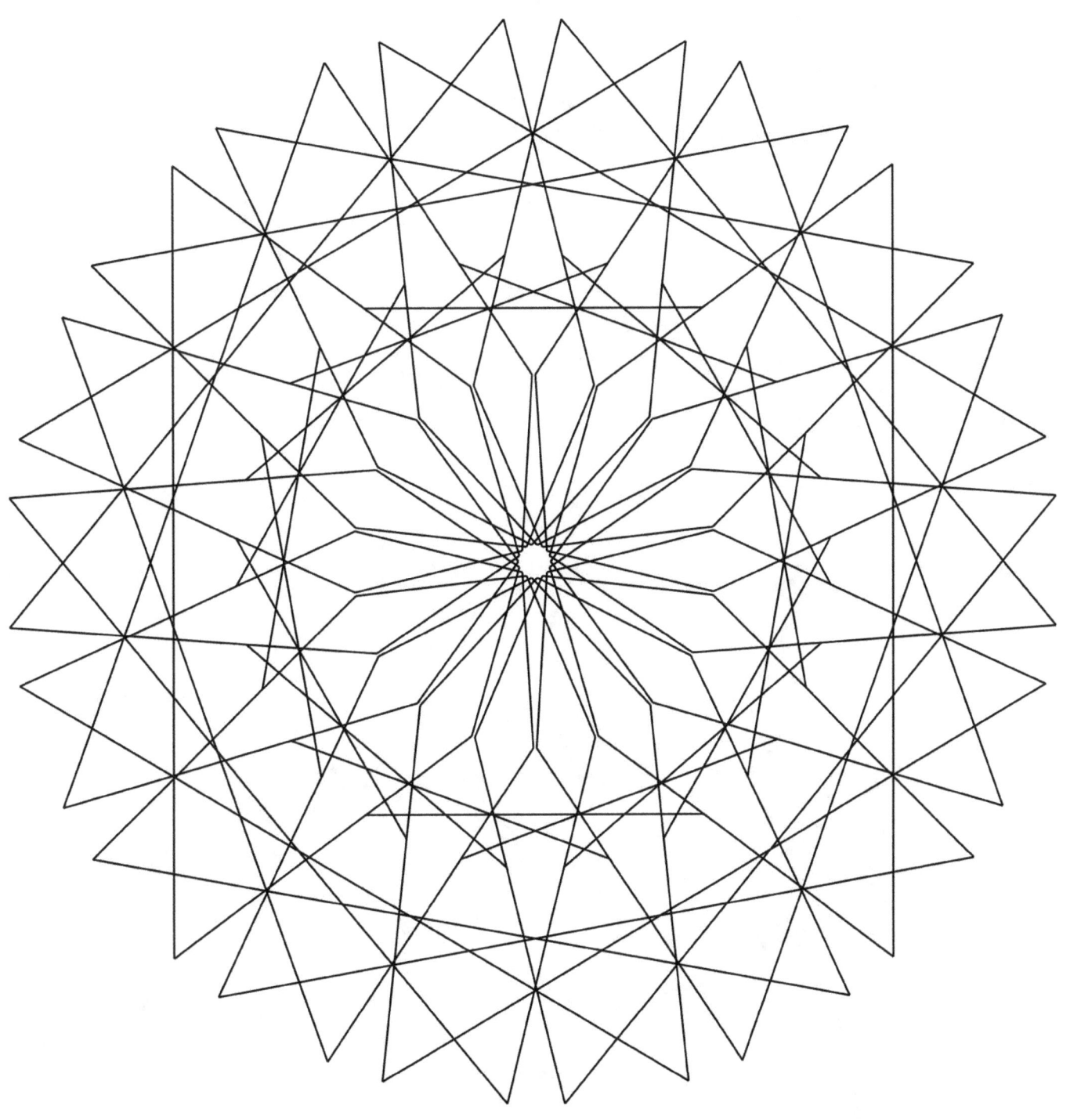

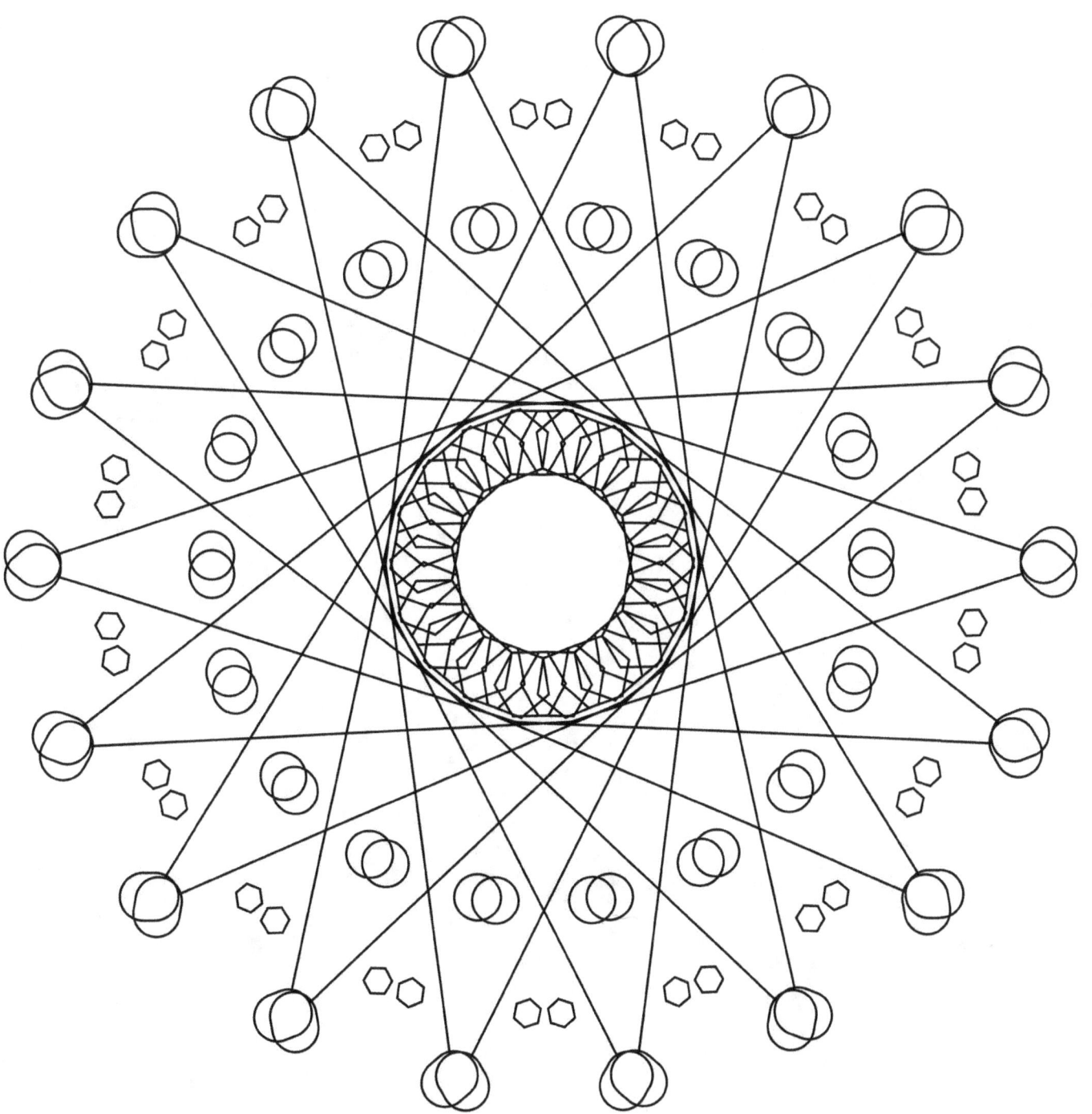

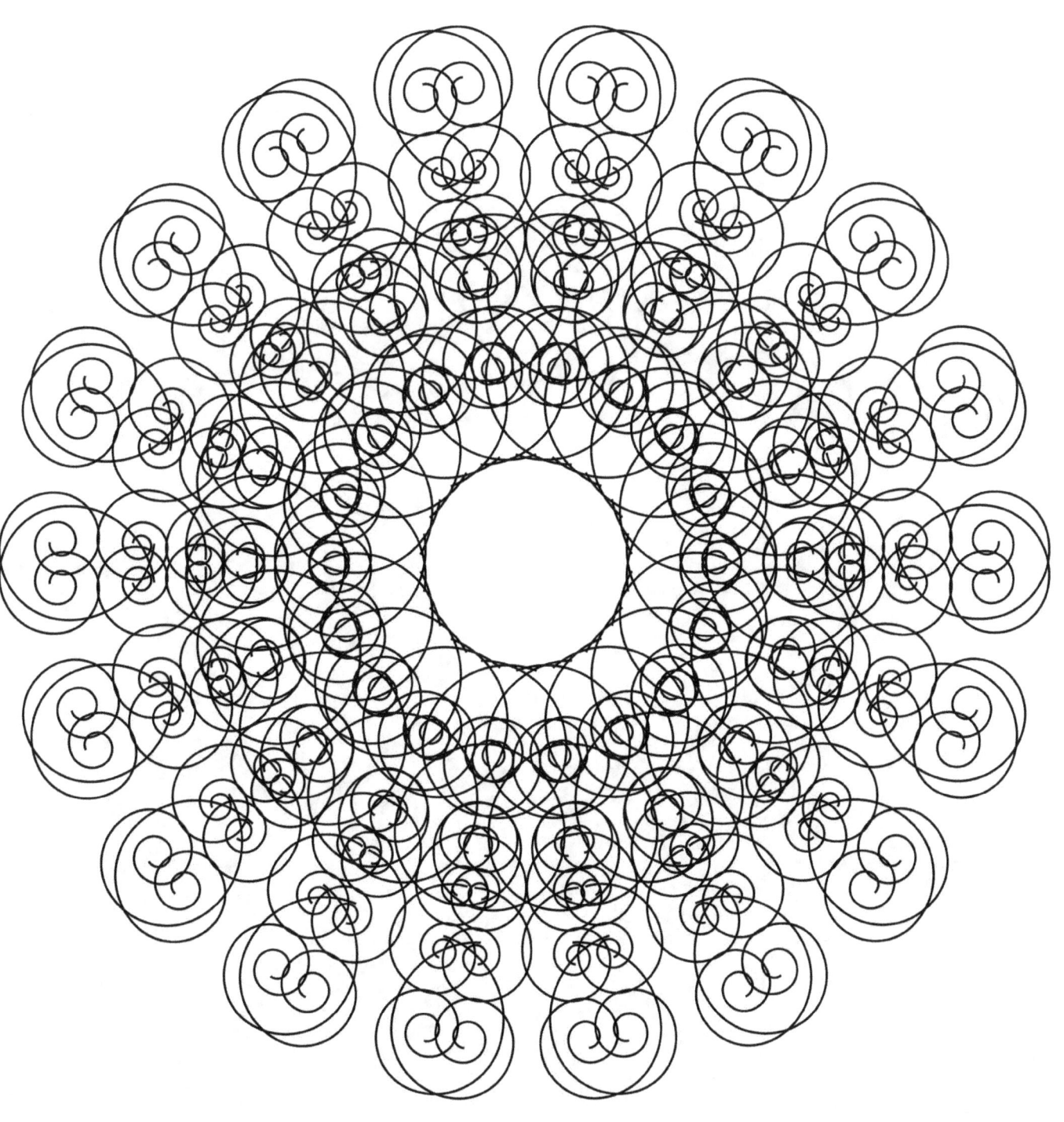

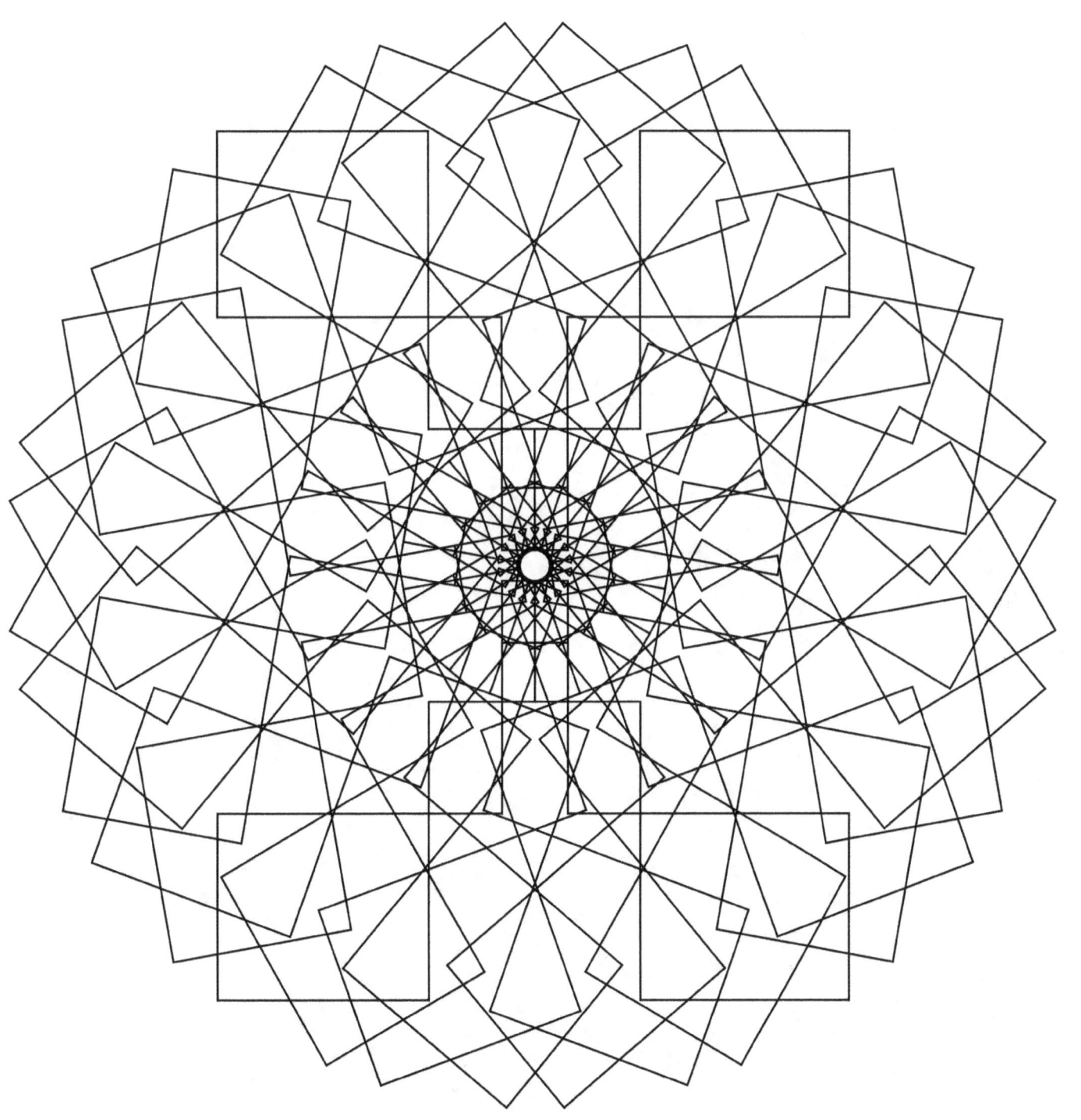

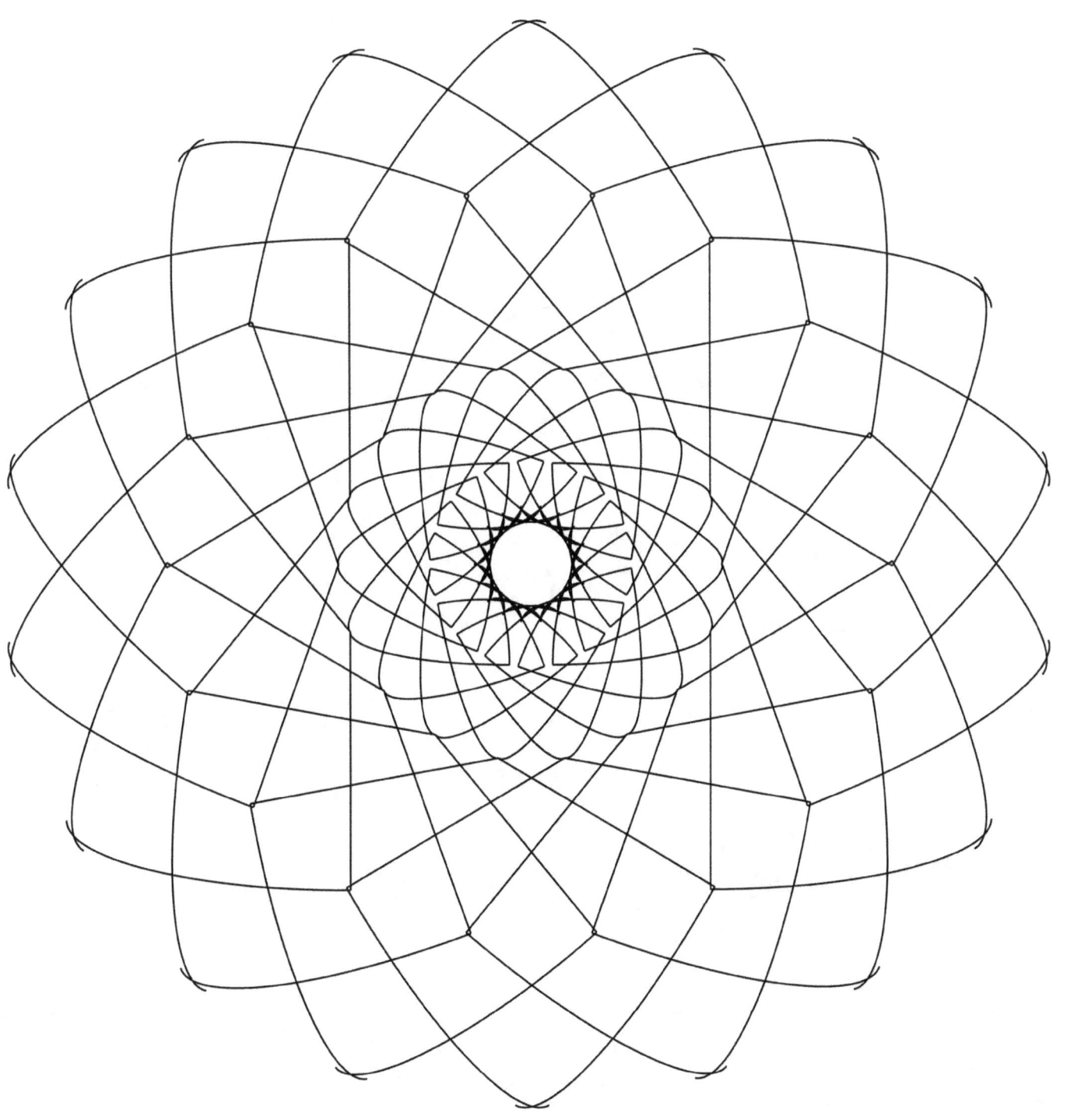

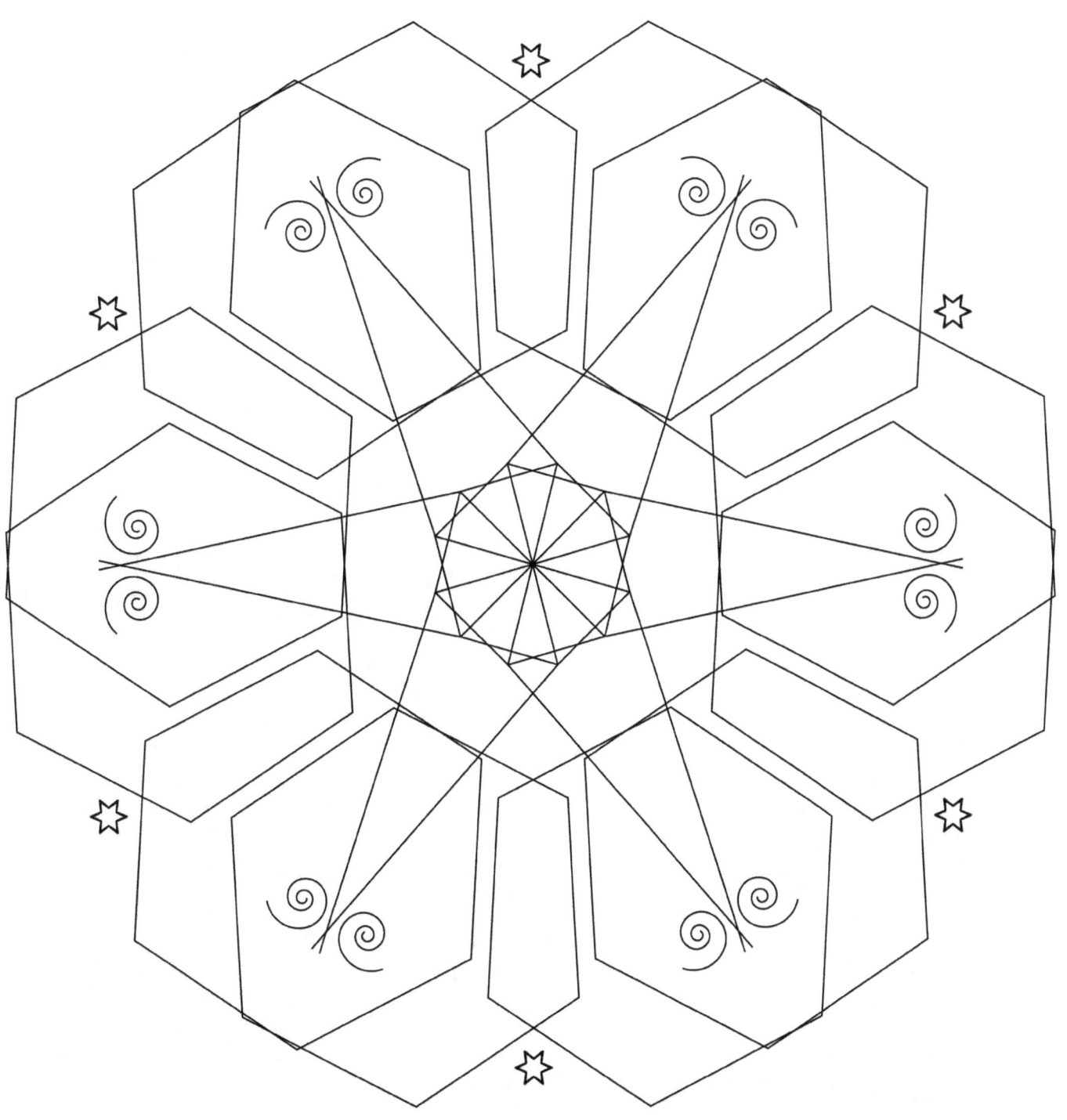

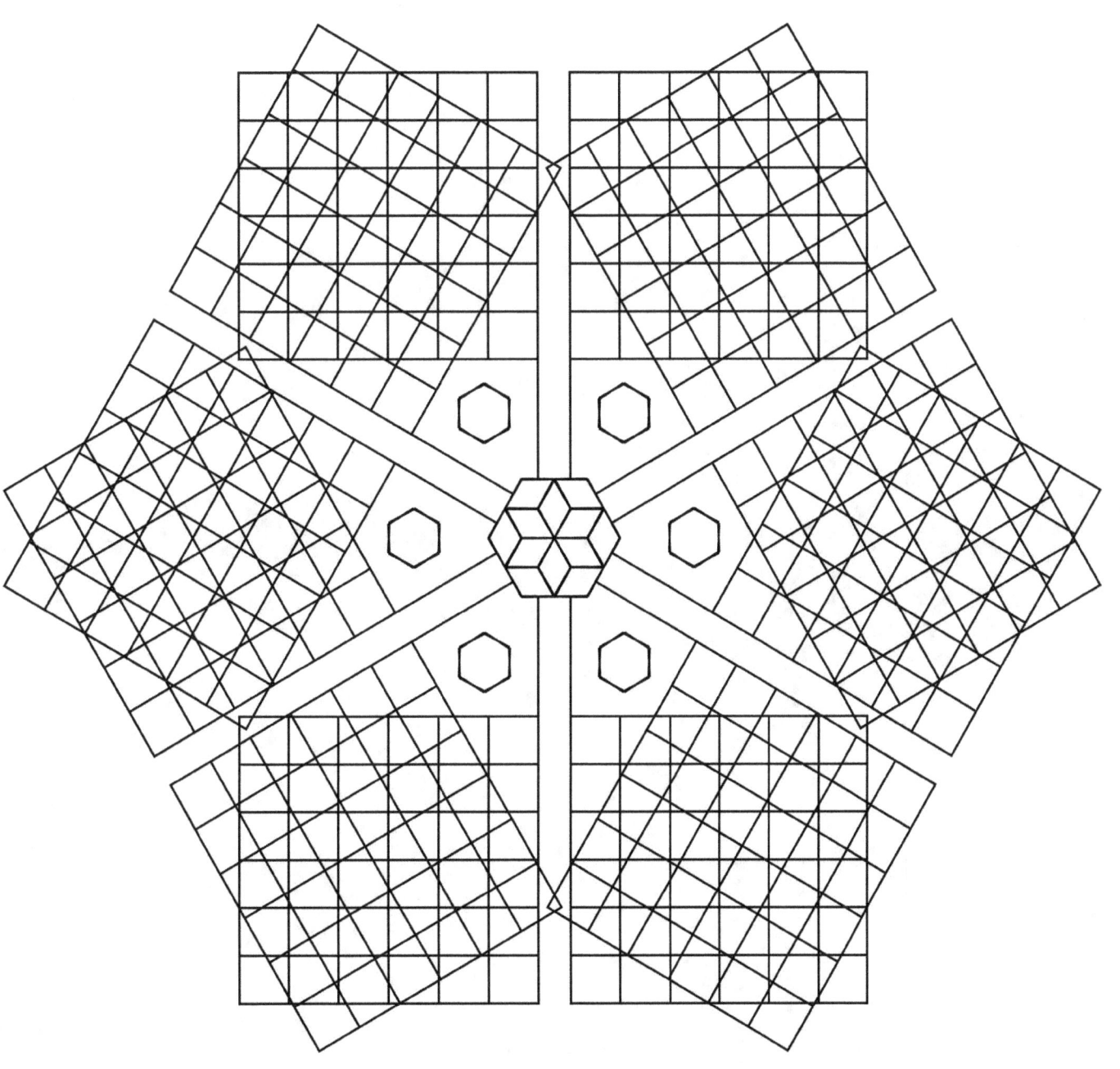

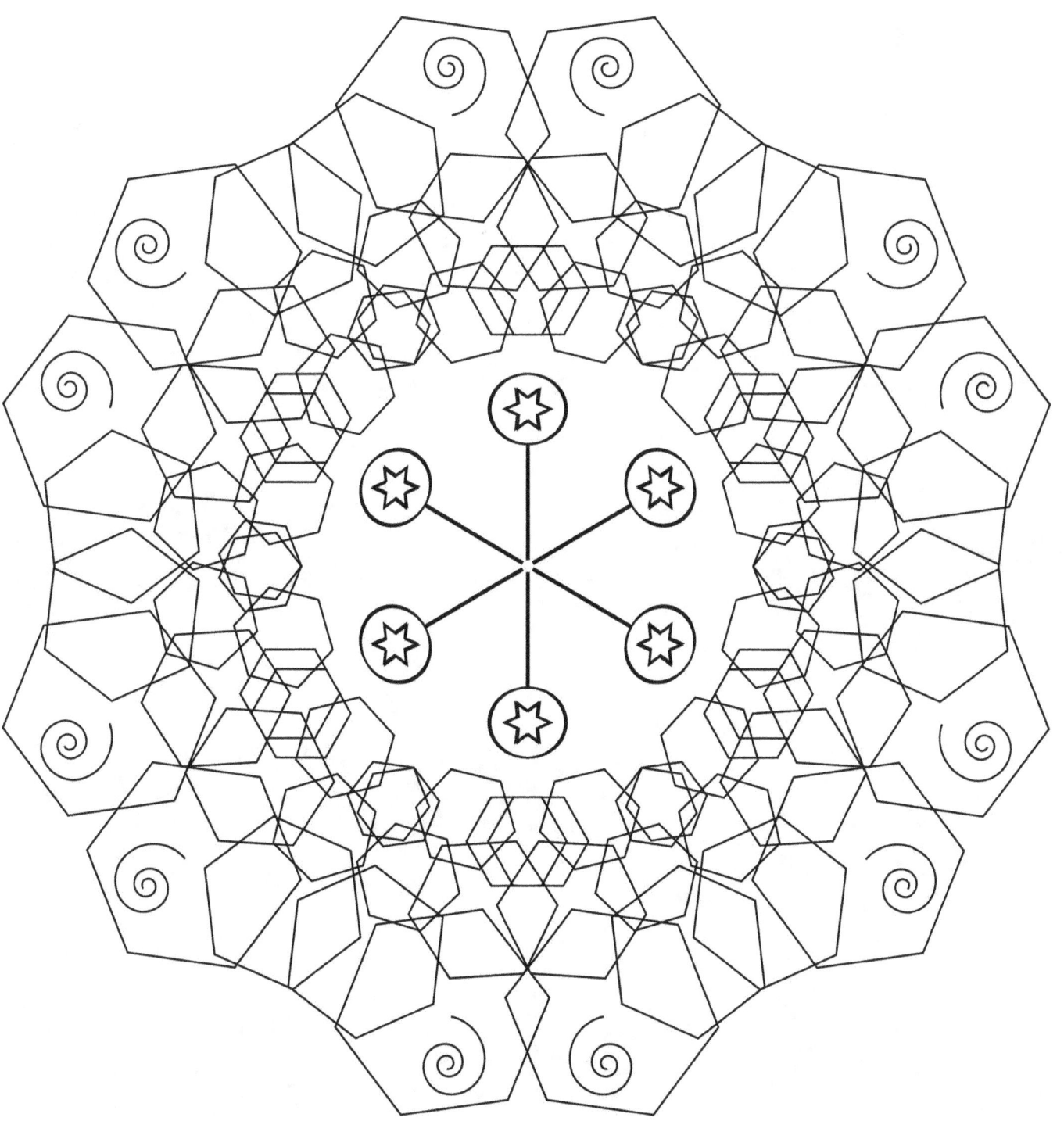

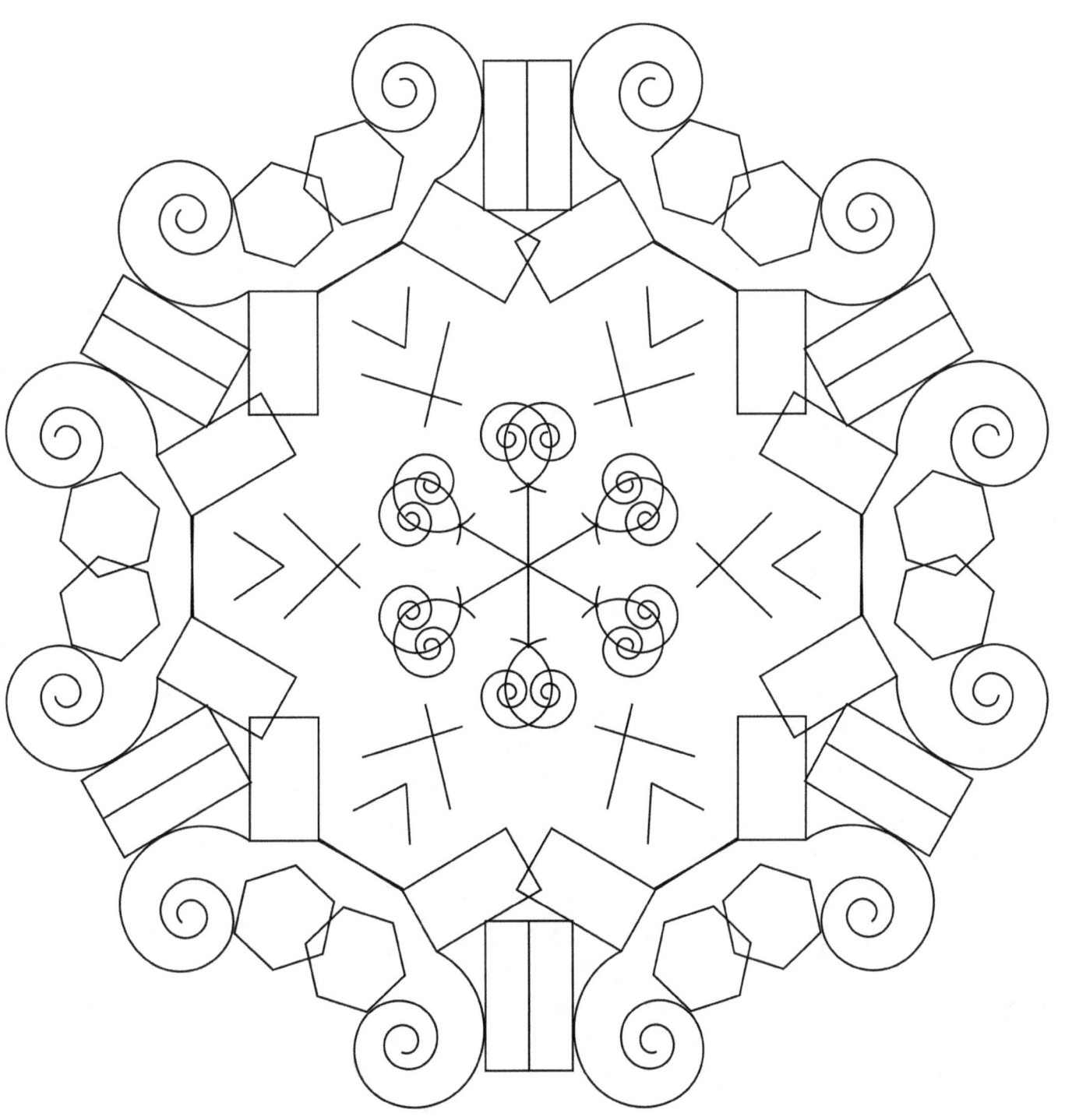

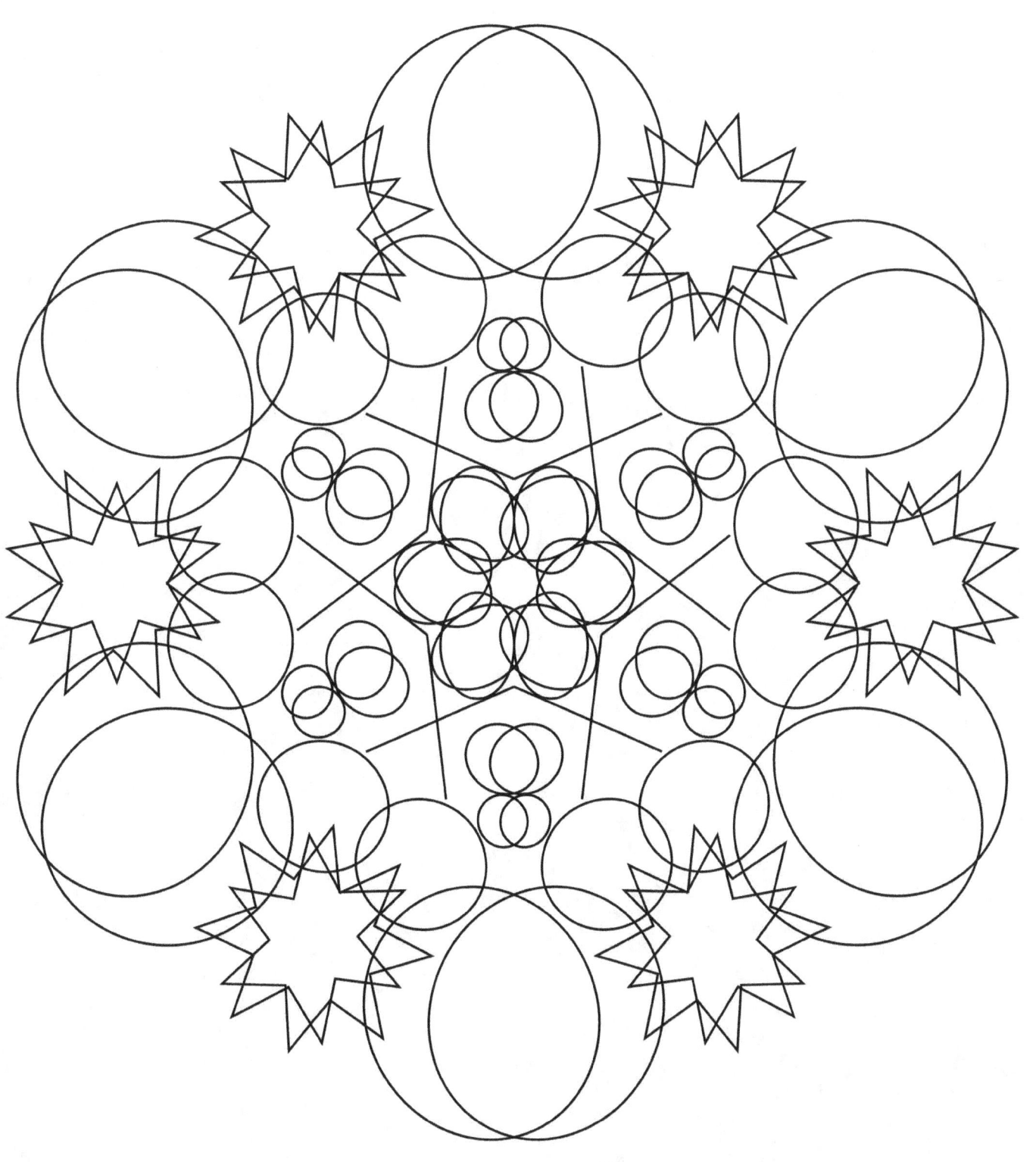

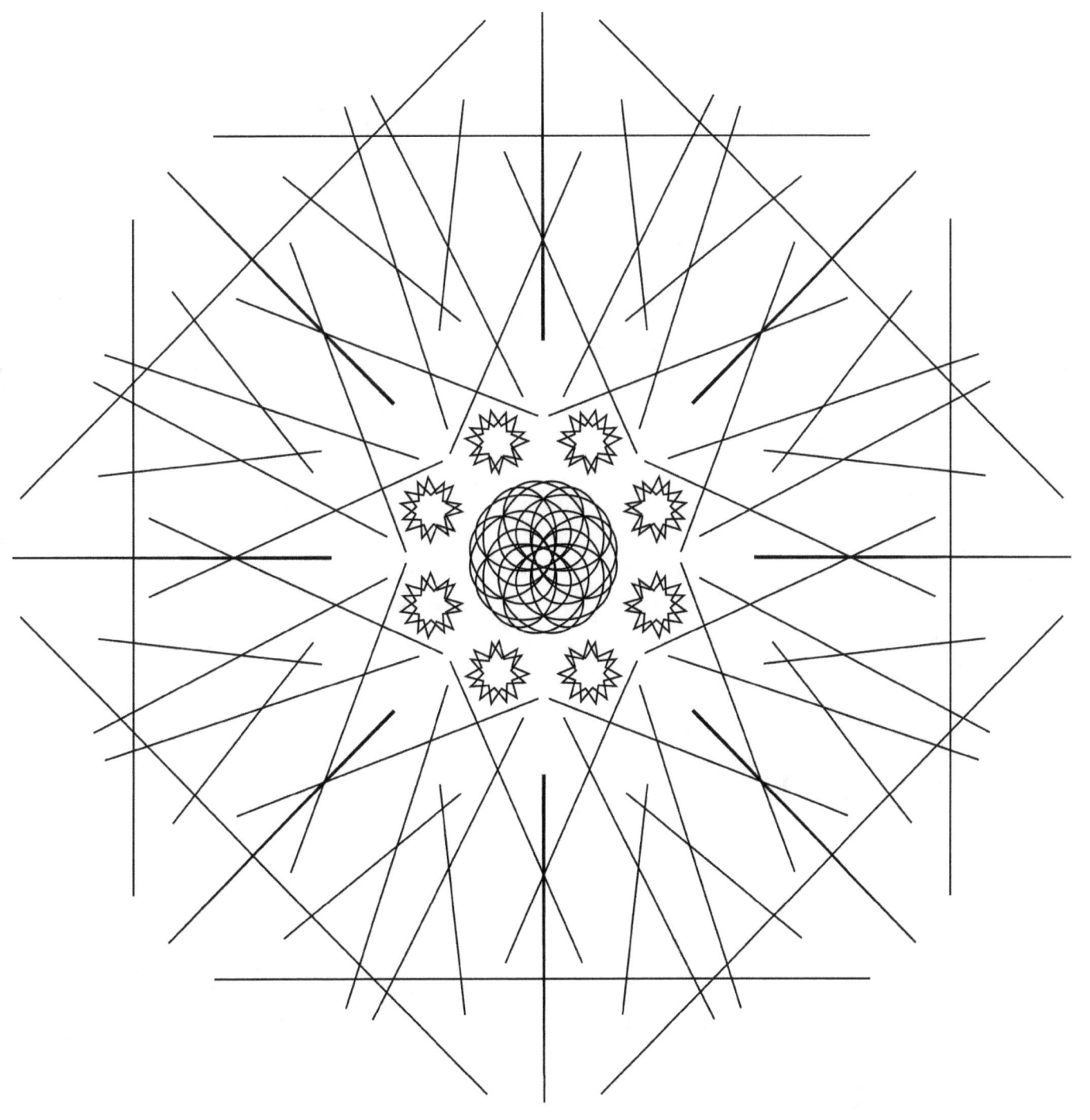

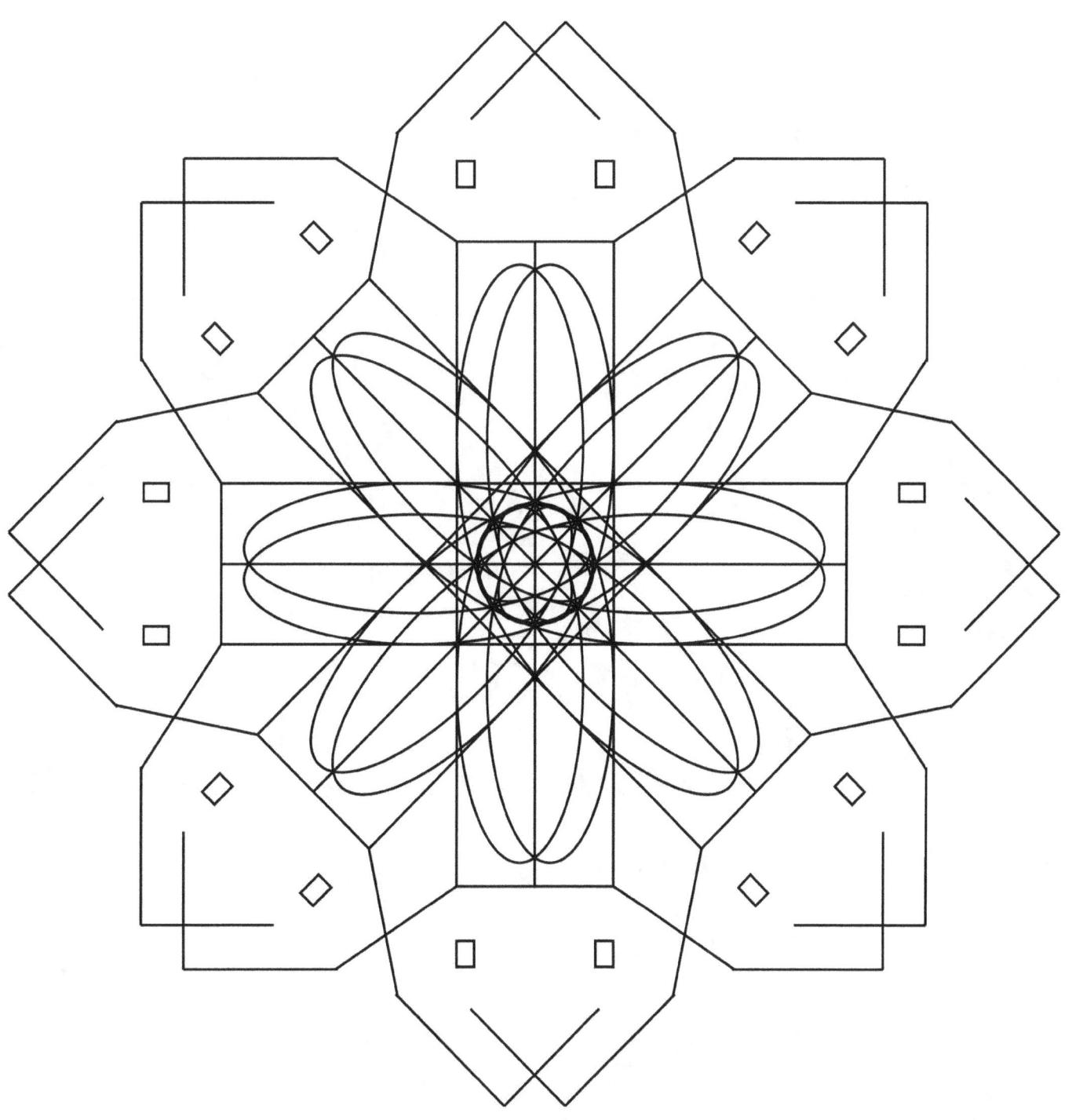

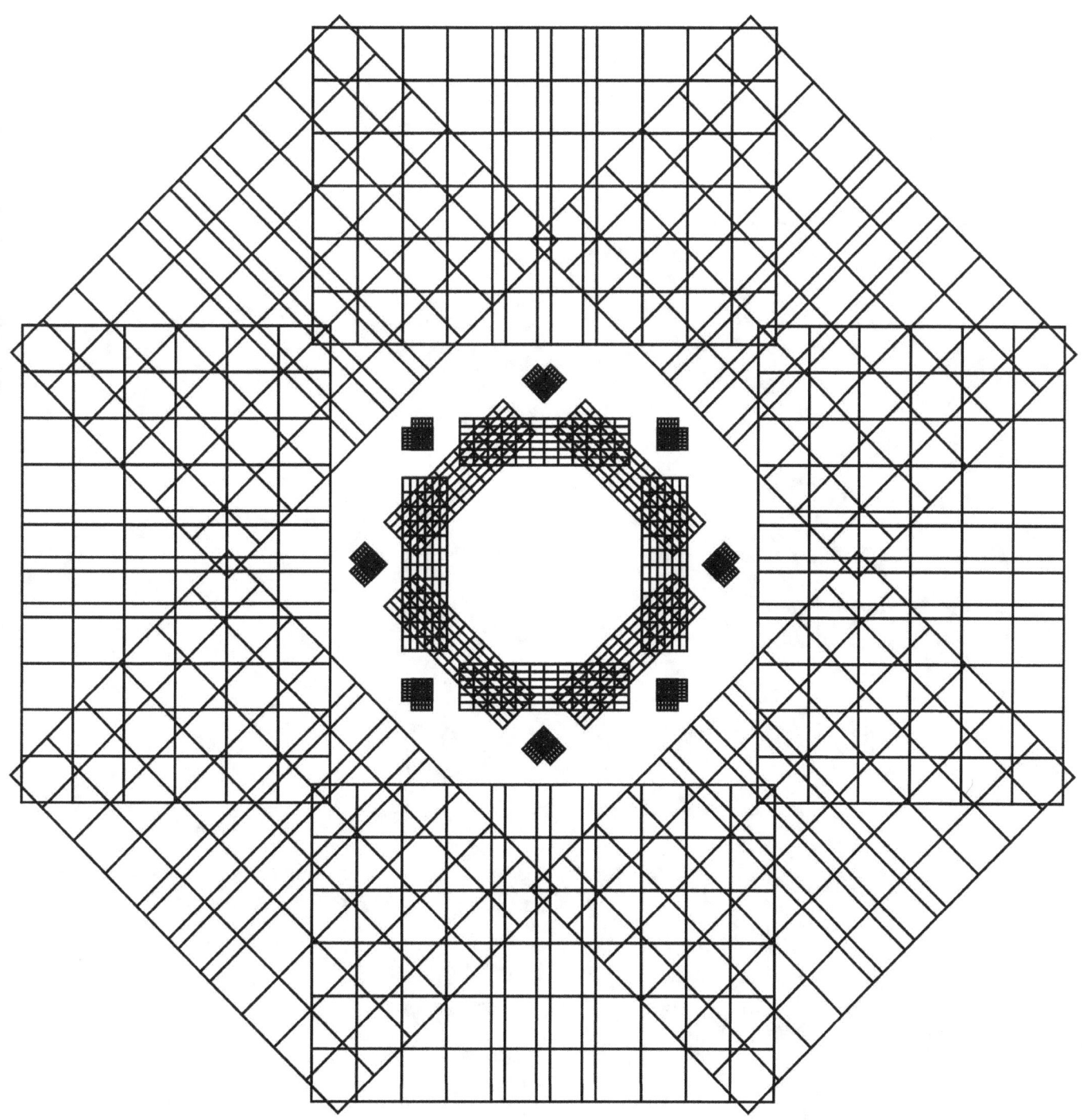

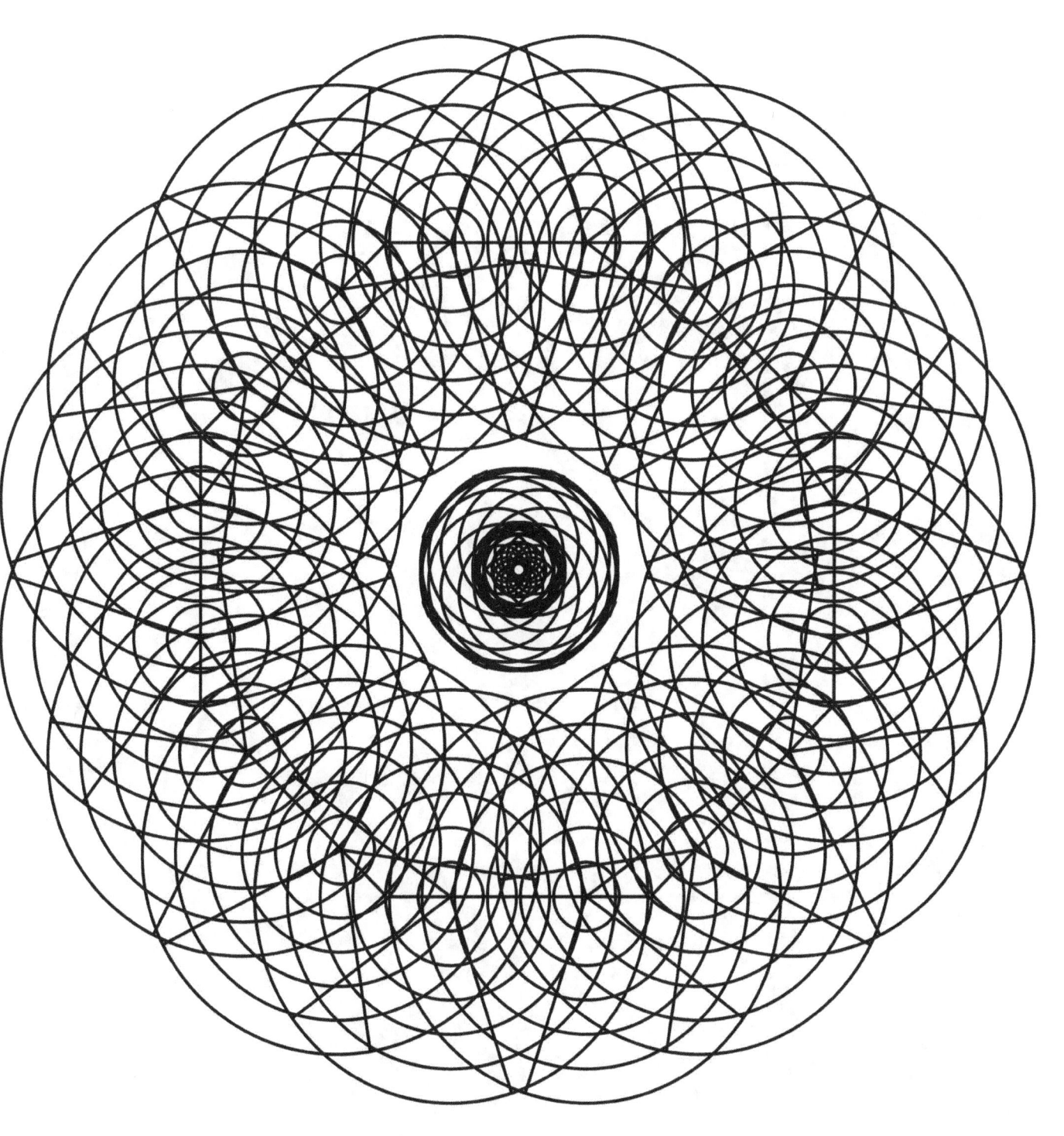

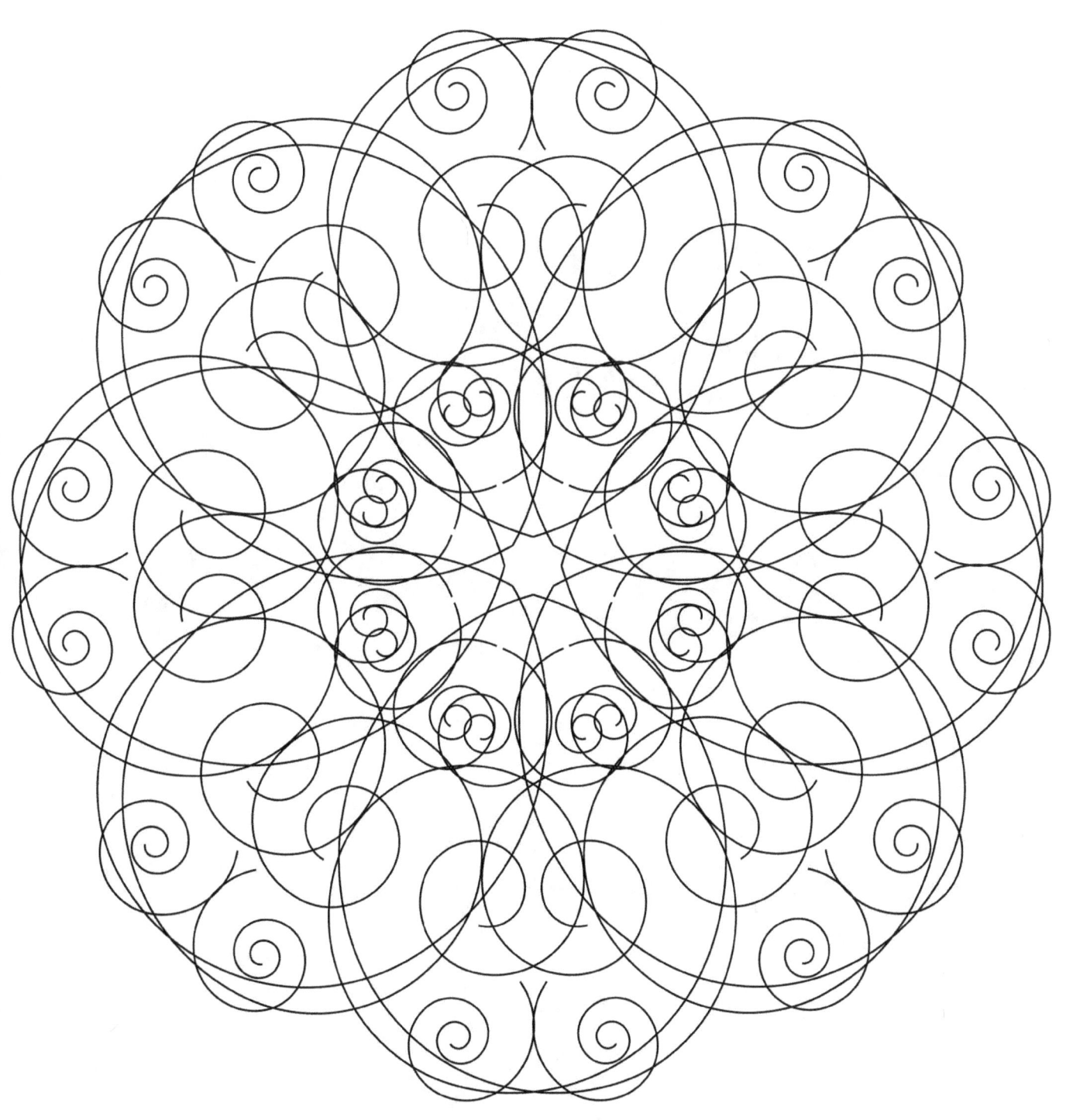

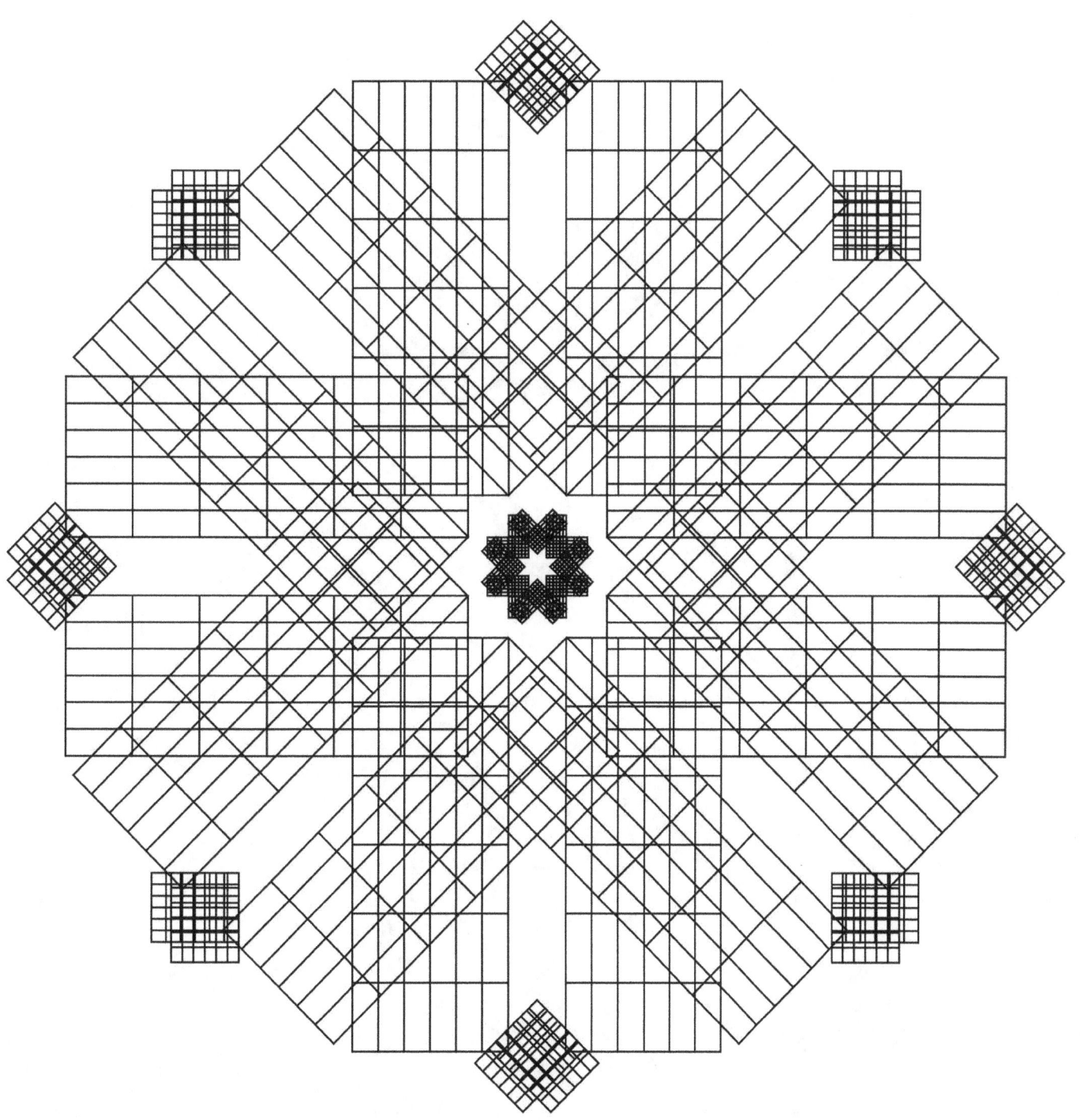

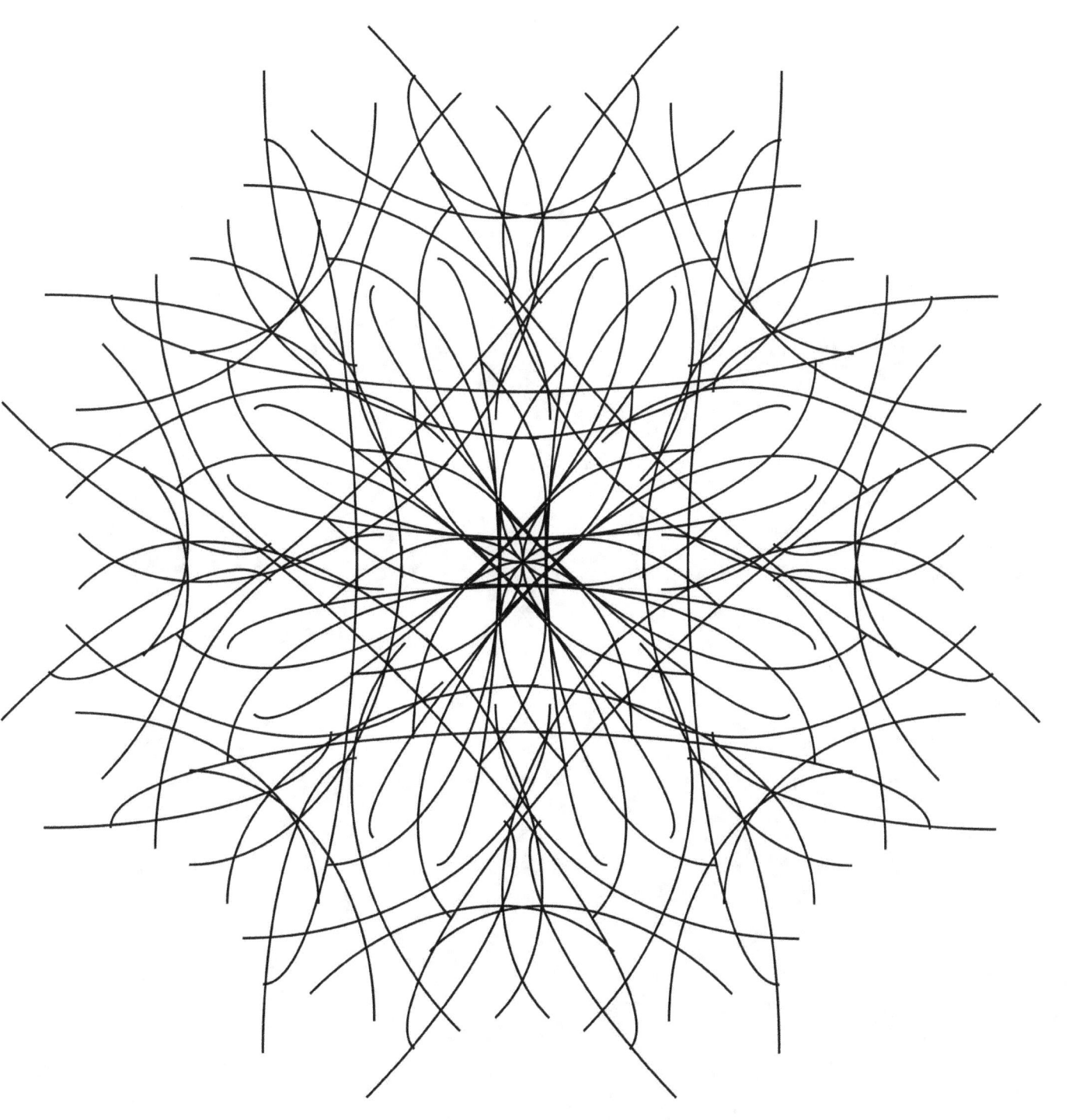

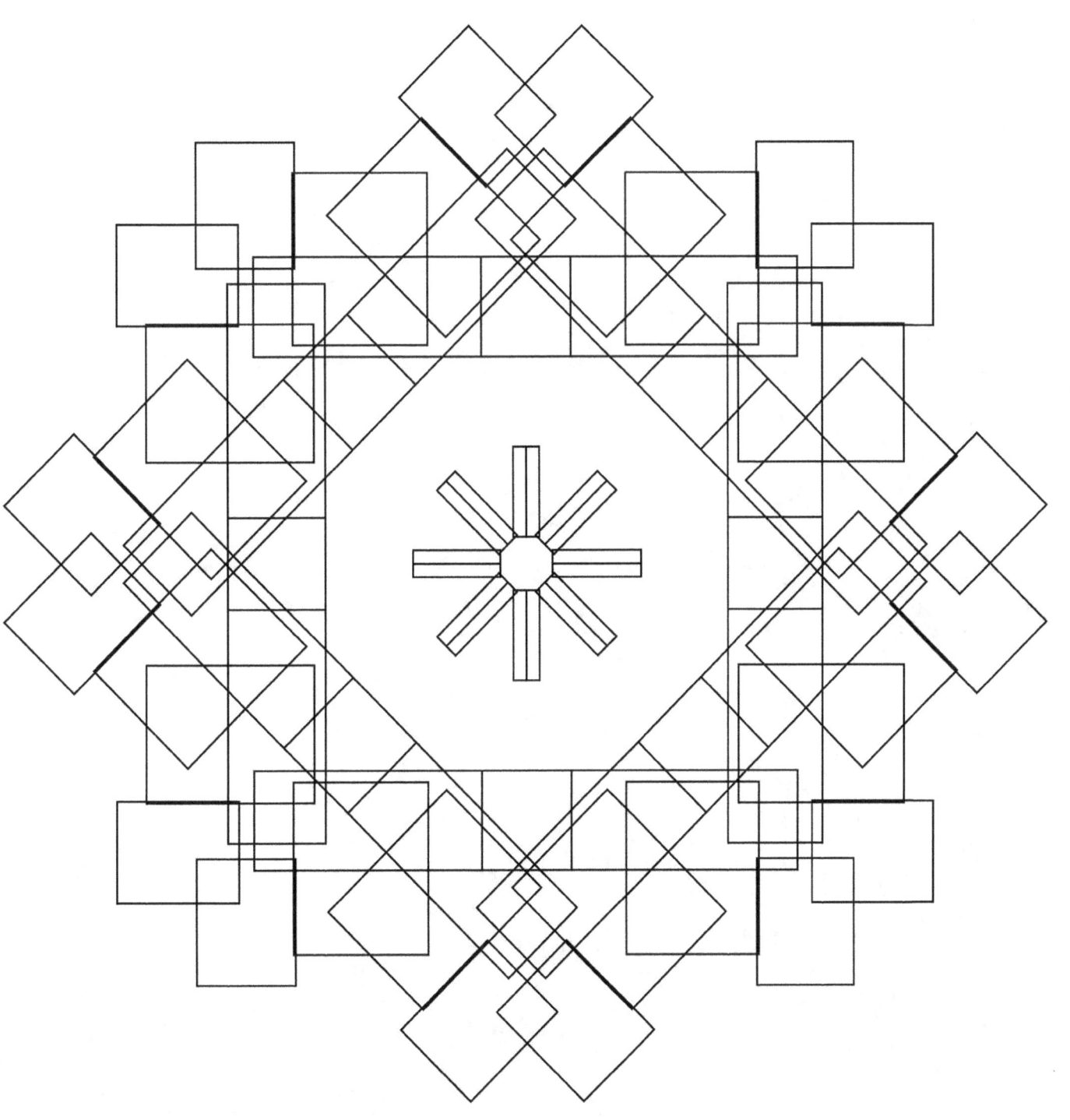

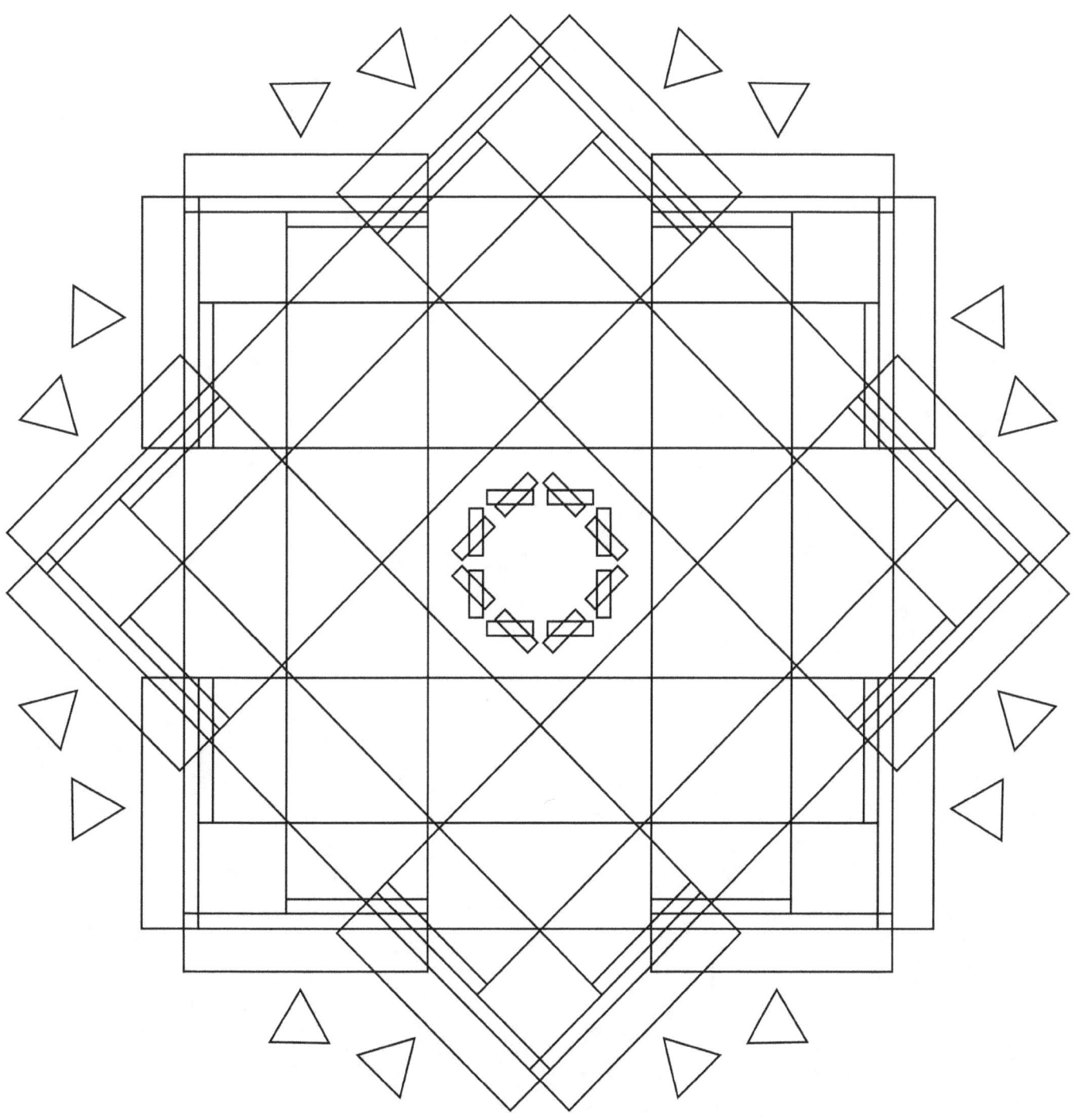

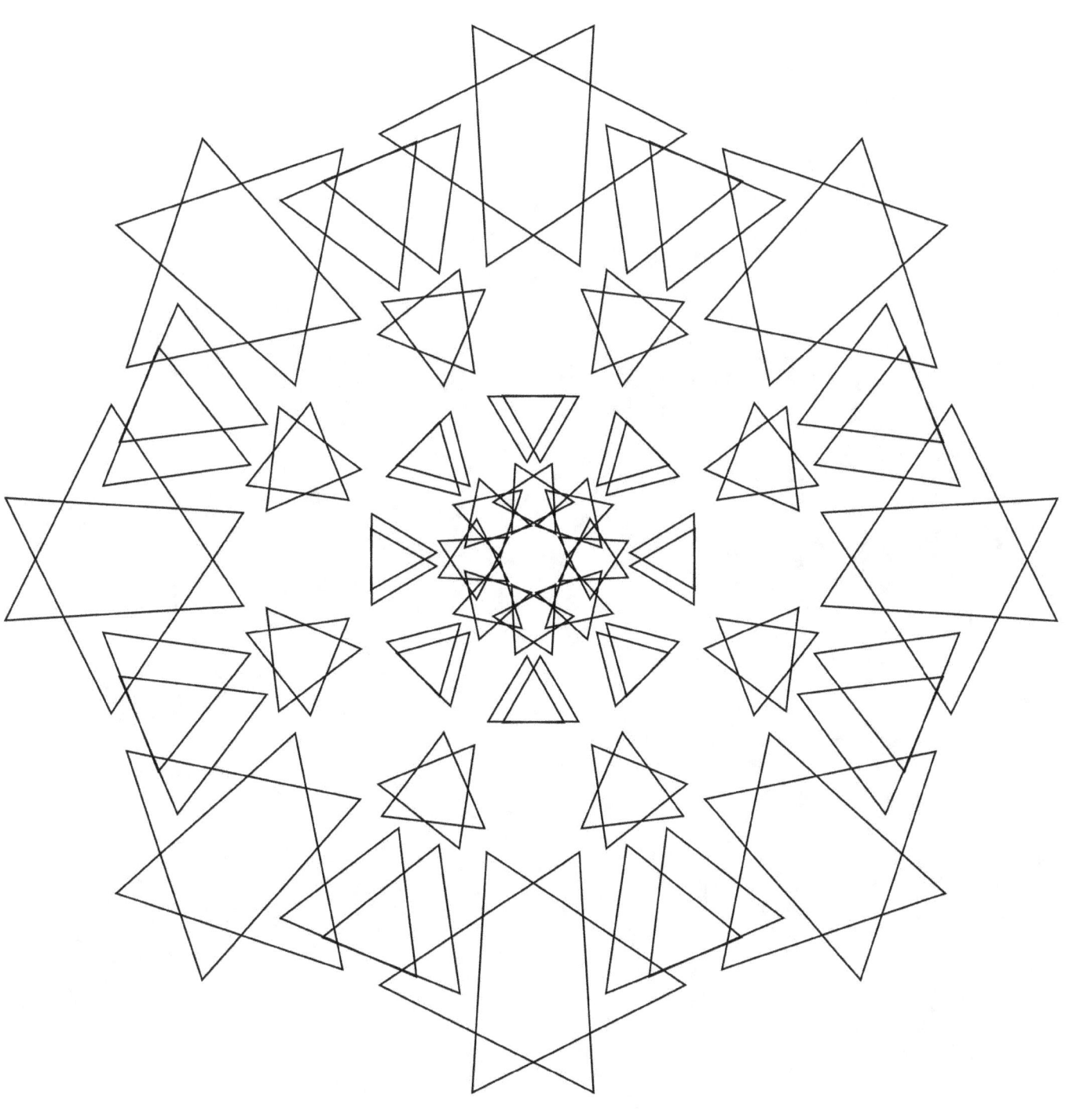

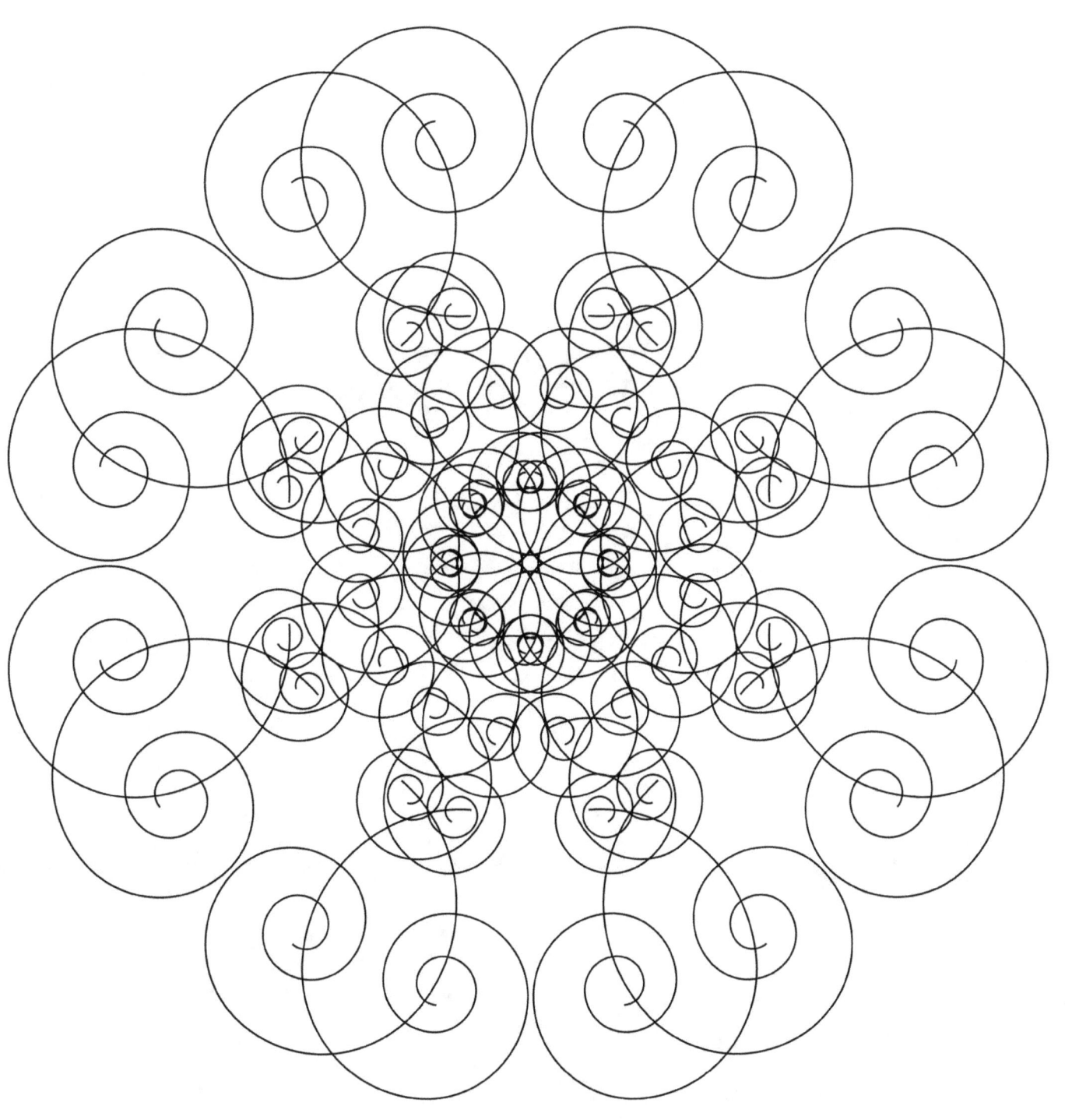

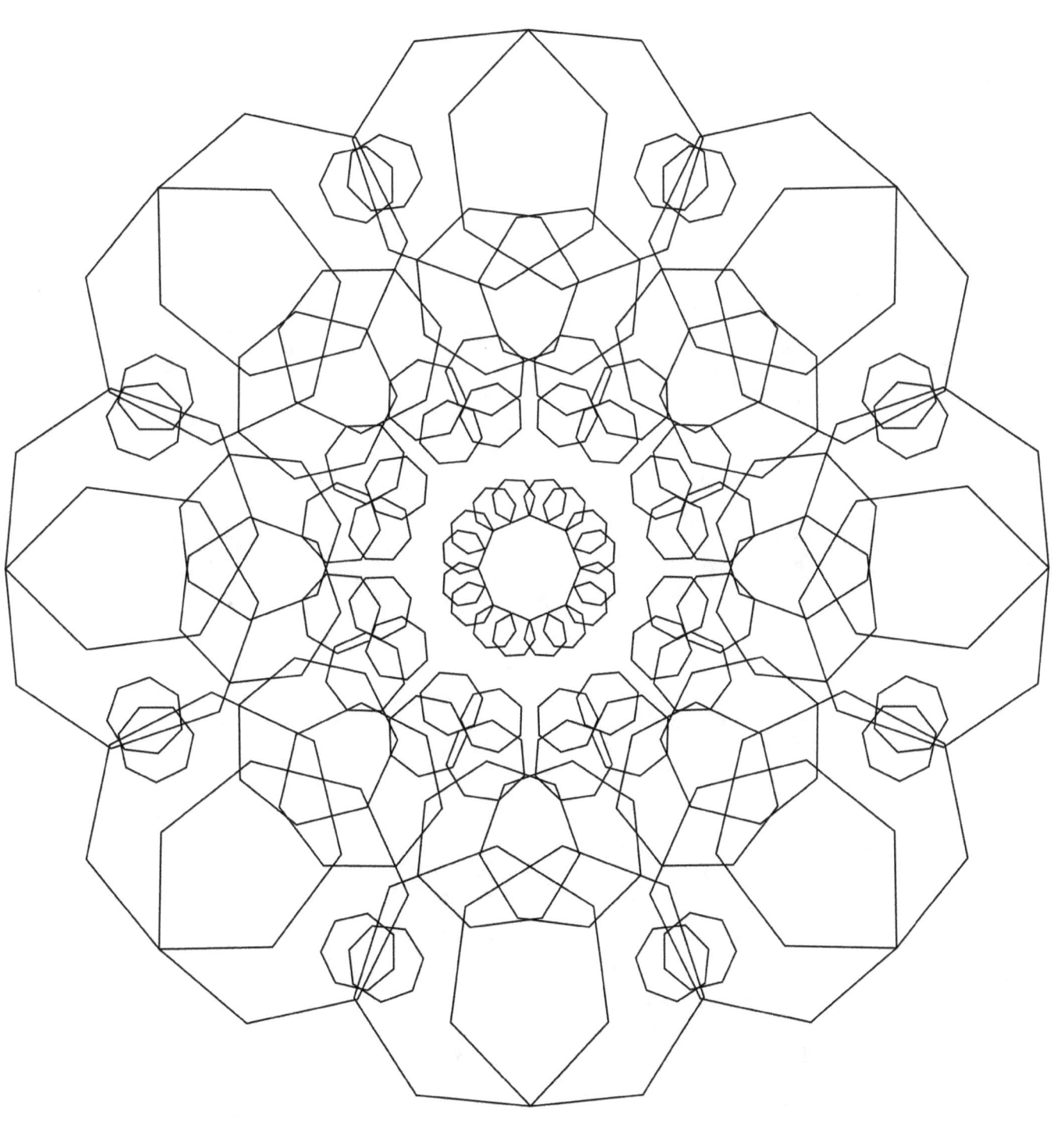

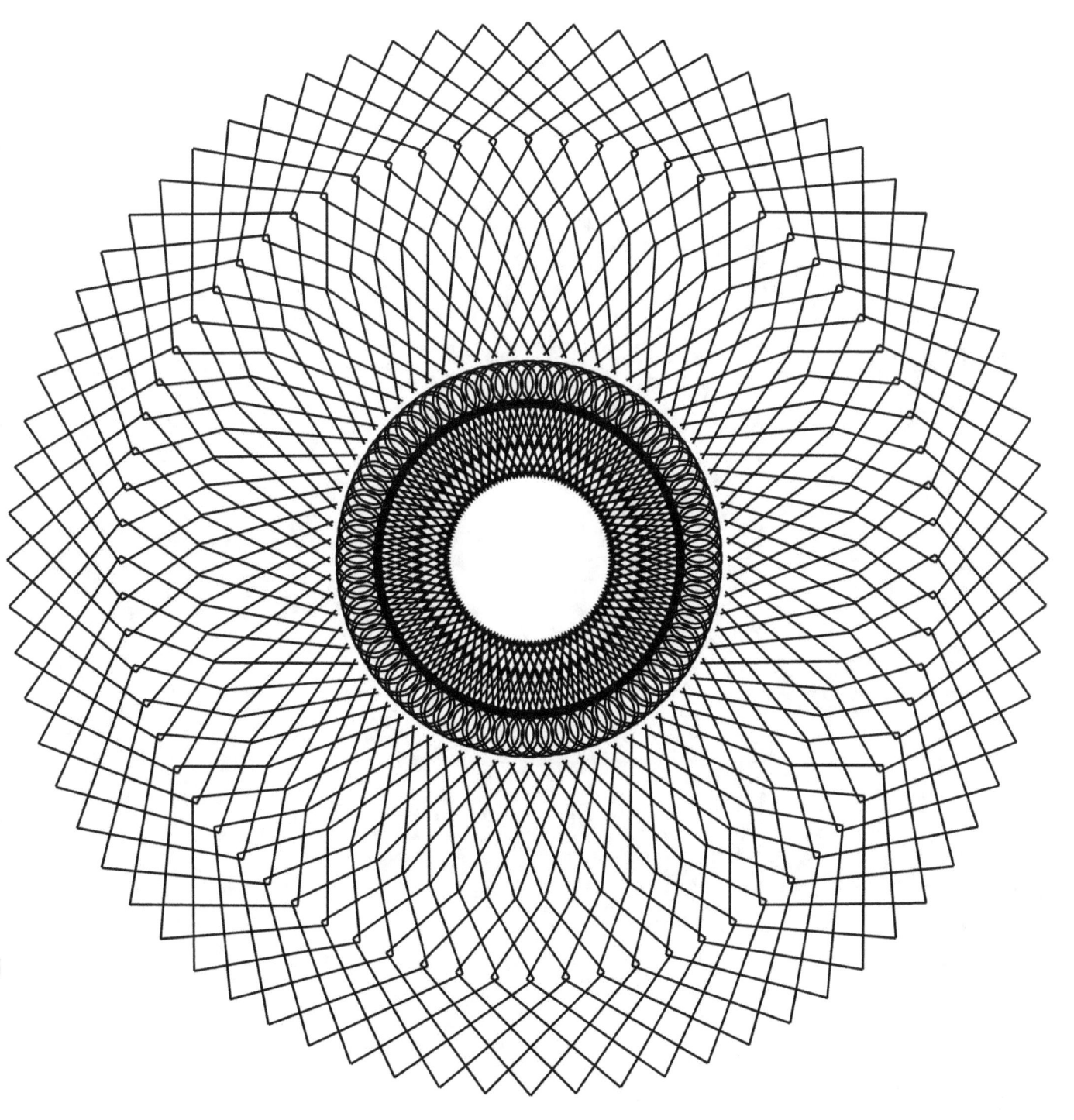